Jung and Swedenborg
on
God and Life After Death

Leon James, Ph.D.

REGENERATION MEDIA
Kailua

God, Immortality and Theistic Psychology Series

www.theisticpsychology.org

This is the Second Edition published in November 2015

Paperback Print and Digital Kindle
ISBN-10: 1517689333
ISBN-13: 978-1517689339
ASIN: B0169SKO98

Table of Contents

Dedication

This book is dedicated to my long time online friend and colleague

Dr. Ian Thompson

Pioneer Physicist in Theistic Science
Exploring theism in philosophy, religion, physics, and psychology

"Theism is the belief that God is the creator and sustainer of the world, and hence of all life and activity within the world, yet in a way whereby the world is as if active from itself."

"Physics and psychology want to know the causes of natural and mental things."

— Ian Thompson

Dr. Thompson's Blog on the Web:
http://blog.beginningtheisticscience.com/

About This Book

The work of Carl Jung (1875-1961) remains an influential presence in psychology today. The Writings of Emanuel Swedenborg (1688-1772) are assuming greater importance in the psychological conception of the human mind. The two together offer a rational and scientific explanation of the collective unconscious and life after death.

Jung's occasional visions of the collective unconscious are supplemented by Swedenborg's permanent state of dual consciousness that he enjoyed for 27 consecutive years. Swedenborg proves by eyewitness reports that the human mind is born immortal and continues life after death in its spiritual body. Jung's description of the process of self-realization through *individuation* is illustrated by Swedenborg's details about the process of *regeneration*. In both cases, human personality development starts in this life at birth and continues in the afterlife to eternity. The mental health of the individual in the afterlife is dependent on acquiring in this life altruistic concerns and habits of positive thinking and interacting with others. This requires that we harness the powerful psychic forces that influence our personality development and ultimately determine our eternal fate.

Fear of death is overcome by the knowledge of immortality.

This book is about afterlife lifestyles. Readers are given actual details about the full course of the personality from our birth to death and beyond. For most people today almost nothing is known about "the beyond". This gives an urgent importance today to the spiritual psychology of Jung and Swedenborg. They have given empirical and experiential verification of life after death and the immortality of our individual personality.

From the vast quantity of the collected works from these two giants, this book extracts little discussed ideas and almost ignored confirmations that Jung and Swedenborg provide regarding the psychology of personality viewed as being immortal.

Jung talked to the "departed" from whom he obtained much information about the collective unconscious in which they existed eternally apart from time. Jung insisted on the critical importance of the individual conscious to learn about how the psychic forces of the collective unconscious influence and control the person's destiny and mental health. Swedenborg had dual consciousness for 27 years continuously, so that he was able to explore the spiritual world of the afterlife and to publish several volumes of ethnographic reports about life in the psychic communities of the spiritual world in the afterlife. Everyone joins one of these psychic societies following the 48-hour dying-resuscitation process in which the physical body is detached from the spiritual body. Swedenborg personally went through that anatomical procedure several times so that he may describe it in detail as a subject. He also interviewed many of the inhabitants of psychic societies, some who were in heavenly states, while others were in their hell.

Never before or since has such clear empirical information about the afterlife come to light in science and psychology.

Taken together the psychology of personality of Jung and Swedenborg offer unique new features of the self and consciousness. Human beings are born into eternity with a spiritual body that is immortal and contains the structural anatomical organs of the mind. Specifically, (1) the affective-circulatory system that provides us with feelings, motives, and emotions, (2) the cognitive-pulmonary system that provides us with thoughts, meanings, and rationality, and (3) the sensorimotor-skeletal-nervous system that provides us with sensations. In the 48-hour dying-resuscitation procedure the temporary material body is detached or expelled and we lose all contact with the physical world. We then continue our immortal personality development living eternally in some suitable psychic society or community.

When we put the spiritual psychology of Jung and Swedenborg together we can see the whole picture of our immortal personality from birth to endless eternity. *What Jung calls our collective unconscious prior to death, Swedenborg calls the collective conscious after death.*

Dying takes us across the barrier between natural and spiritual consciousness.

All spiritual knowledge and all enlightenment of consciousness are available to us now, prior to our death. Jung's collective unconscious and Swedenborg's collective conscious hold the key to our eternal destiny. Now is the time to take charge of our spiritual growth and development process. The quality of happiness in our life on earth and the stability of our mental health, are controlled by powerful psychic forces and societies to which our personality is anatomically connected, both by inheritance and by what we feel attracted to. Knowing this collective interdependency gives us greater control over our mental world, and this has many psychological and emotional benefits. Negative emotions and mood swings can be avoided, which gives the opportunity to acquire positive ways of emoting, thinking, and interacting with others.

After death our mental development compels us to make a choice between letting go of all negativity and holding on to the positive traits that we acquired through lifestyle change efforts. Or else, letting go of all positive traits and holding on to the negative traits embedded in our personality from a lifetime of practice. It is a free choice. Since the choice is made totally in liberty it is love that makes it. What we love most deeply in our personality structure seizes power after death and rearranges the order of affections and preferences, making them compatible with itself. This is called the ruling love and the chief love. When we become conscious of this element in our psyche, we can harness it for the benefit of our further development.

If we do not take charge of our mental growth in a conscious and focused effort we remain such as we were born with the same ruling love dictating our eternal future in the afterlife.

In his role as modern oracle Jung warned that there are dark and powerful psychic forces that are our enemy and seek to destroy people and societies. He insisted that in order to control these negative forces that exist in the collective unconscious, we need to get to know them. This is our only defense. Our spiritual knowledge defeats the psychic forces. *But this knowledge cannot be learned or transmitted, it must be experienced.* Swedenborg gives many details about this interconnection that takes place between independent psychic forces and our individual thoughts and feelings, consequently our happiness and mental health.

This book not only exposes the spiritual psychology of Jung and Swedenborg but also shows the relevance and importance of that psychology for our mental health and functioning, both in this life and in the afterlife. Jung's idea of individuation as self-realization is expanded by Swedenborg's idea of regeneration. Jung's concept of the collective unconscious is expanded by Swedenborg's ethnographic description of the psychic societies in the afterlife who live in collective consciousness as a community, and simultaneously as well as an individual or ego-consciousness that has unique reactions and understanding.

We have the capacity to influence now the choice of which society shall be our home forever. That is the practical and spiritual importance of this book.

About The Author

The author Dr. Leon James is a professor of psychology at the University of Hawaii where he has taught for forty years. He has published articles and books in his academic specialty areas that include spiritual psychology, driving psychology, language teaching, psycholinguistics, information science, and theistic psychology. He is on the editorial board of various academic journals in psychology, and is a regular consultant on road rage to community, government, and safety organizations. Since 1996 he has given over 1,500 interviews on road rage to reporters and news media.

Email: leon@hawaii.edu

Web site on Theistic Psychology: http://theisticpsychology.org/

Psychology is a preparation for death. We have an urge to leave life at a higher level than the one at which we entered. ~Carl Jung; Conversations with C.G. Jung, Psychotherapy, Page 16.

Chapter 1
Jung's Relationship to Swedenborg

Swedenborg's Influence on Some Well Known Writers

Emanuel Swedenborg (1688-1772) has had a remarkable story in the history of literary and scientific literature. No other author has been acclaimed as the greatest genius by so many well-known and influential writers in Western literature. This is clear from the list below. And yet there is no mention of Swedenborg in the history books of psychology and social science. Today there is increasing interest in Swedenborg's Writings as indicated by a Web search on his name, which yields more than half a million results (compared to 25 million for Jung and 19 million for Freud).

Swedenborg's Writings present a radically new psychology of the human mind based on his empirical observations during his mental state of dual consciousness that he enjoyed for 27 years 24/7. He presents extensive ethnographic reports of the life and communities in the spiritual world, which he defines as the afterlife of eternity. He describes death as a dying-resuscitation process that takes two days, after which the individual becomes conscious in the spiritual body and continues unending life thereafter. People live in psychic communities, gathering together in accordance with the compatibility of their personality structure. Swedenborg reports conversations he had with many of the well-known writers of antiquity with whom he was familiar from the literature. He reports carrying out regular conversations with his acquaintances just two days after they passed on.

Some critics of Swedenborg's reports of the afterlife have simply labeled him as psychotic or delusional. Others have seen in his works as a new religion. Still others, like those listed below, have seen him as remarkable genius. This high assessment is due not so much to his visions per se as to his rational presentation of the dual world and how it affects our mind and development. In Swedenborg's Writings they find a novel, coherent and systematic explanation of reality, God, life after death, and the nature of the human mind. Here is one list with about 40 entries:

Honoré de Balzac (1799-1850)
French novelist; declared that Swedenborgianism was his religion.

Charles Baudelaire (1821-1867)
French poet; fascinated by Swedenborg's doctrine of 'correspondences'; used this as a cornerstone of his aesthetic metaphysics.

William Blake (1757-1827)
Poet and artist; called Swedenborg a "divine teacher".

Elizabeth Barrett Browning (1806-1861) and Robert Browning (1812-1889)
Renowned English poets read Swedenborg's Conjugial Love together in Florence early in their marriage.

Thomas Carlyle (1795-1881)
Eminent Scottish essayist; described Swedenborg as 'one of the spiritual suns that will shine brighter as the years go on.'

Fyodor Dostoevsky (1821-1881)
Great Russian novelist; his books contain clear Swedenborgian teaching about the spiritual world, particularly that hell is always a voluntary spiritual state.

Ralph Waldo Emerson (1803-1882)
American poet, philosopher and essayist; His biographical essay, 'Swedenborg, or the Mystic' was published in his Representative Men.

Johann Wolfgang von Goethe (1749-1832)
Great German poet, dramatist, novelist, essayist and scientist; students of his letters and poetry have found evidence of familiarity with both scientific and theological works of Swedenborg)

Immanuel Kant (1724-1804)
(great German Idealist philosopher became aware of Swedenborg's reputation as a clairvoyant and seer in the early 1760s; wrote a frequently cited scathing attack on Swedenborg entitled Dreams of a Spirit-Seer (1766)

Joseph Sheridan Le Fanu (1814-1873)
(Anglo-Irish novelist and short-story writer; made his living as a journalist; Swedenborg's influence on his writing may be seen most strongly in his best-known novel Uncle Silas)

Oscar V de Lubicz Milosz (1877-1939)
Lithuanian diplomat and French poet, he was one of the last great hermetic thinkers of the twentieth century and a student of Swedenborg.

George MacDonald (1824-1905)
Scottish novelist, poet and 'myth-maker'; inspired by Swedenborg and Blake.

Czeslaw Milosz (1911-2004)
Lithuanian-born poet, novelist, essayist, translator, critic and scholar; won the Nobel Prize for Literature in 1980; acknowledged Swedenborg

as one of his main sources of inspiration.

Coventry Patmore (1823-1896)
English poet; was inspired by his reading of Swedenborg's Conjugial
Love; acknowledges the influence of Swedenborg on his work and may
be seen in his later volume The Unknown Eros.

Arthur Schopenhauer (1788-1860)
German Idealist philosopher; fascinated by Swedenborg and employs
terminology in relation to the connection between the will and the
understanding.

DT Suzuki (1870-1966)
Internationally known Japanese Zen Buddhist scholar; translated into
Japanese several Swedenborg books; described Swedenborg as 'the
Buddha of the North'.

Alfred Lord Tennyson (1809-1892)
Most popular poet of the Victorian age; lifelong reader of Swedenborg.

Walt Whitman (1819-1892)
Leading American poet of the nineteenth century; wrote that Swedenborg
will probably 'make the deepest and broadest mark upon the religions of
future ages here, of any man that ever walked the earth.'

James John Garth Wilkinson (1812-1899)
(Homoeopathic physician, translator and biographer of Swedenborg and
a writer on a variety of religious, medical and social topics)

Calvin Coolidge, American President (1872-1933)
"I desire to express my deep interest in the work and life of this
advanced scientist and thinker Swedenborg, who was a pioneer two
hundred years ago in much of the progress and advancement in
mechanical, biological and medical science of the present day, and
whose great learning and deep understanding of the mysteries of life
was supplemented by the strong religious faith which has had devout
followers many generations after the founder's death."

Helen Keller, Author (1880-1968)
I acknowledge my profound indebtedness to Emanuel Swedenborg

for a richer interpretation of the Bible, a deeper understanding of Christianity, and a precious sense of the divine presence in the world. His message has meant so much to me. It has given color and reality and unity to my thought of the life to come; it has exalted my ideas of love, truth and usefulness; it has been my strongest incitement to overcome limitations. Swedenborg's Divine Love and Wisdom is a fountain of life I am always happy to be near."

Dr. Carl Gustav Jung, Psychologist (1875-1961)
"I admire Swedenborg as a great scientist and a great mystic at the same time. His life and work has always been of great interest to me and I read about seven fat volumes of his writings when I was a medical student."

Henry James Sr., Author (1811-1882)
"Emanuel Swedenborg had the sanest and most far-reaching intellect this age has ever known."

William Butler Yeats, Poet (1865-1939)
"It was indeed Swedenborg who affirmed for the modern world, as against the abstract reasoning of the learned, the doctrine and practice of the desolate places, of shepherds and midwives, and discovered a world of spirits where there was a scenery like that of the earth, human forms, grotesque or beautiful, senses that knew pleasure and pain, marriage and war, all that could be painted upon canvas or put into stories."

Sir Arthur Conan Doyle, Author (1859-1930)
"The great Swedish seer Emanuel Swedenborg has some claim to be the father of our new knowledge of supernal matters. When the first rays of the rising sun of spiritual knowledge fell upon the earth they illuminated the greatest and highest human mind before they shed their light on lesser men. That mountain peak of mentality was this great religious reformer and clairvoyant medium..."

Samuel Taylor Coleridge, Poet (1772-1834)
"Of the too limited time which my ill-health and the exigencies of the today leave in my power, I have given the larger portion to the works of Swedenborg. I remember nothing in Lord Bacon superior, few passages equal, either in depth of thought, or in richness, dignity and

felicity of diction, or in the weightiness of the truths contained in these articles. I can venture to assert that as a moralist Swedenborg is above all praise; and that as a naturalist, psychologist and theologian, he has strong and varied claims on the gratitude and admiration of the professional and philosophical world."

Jorge Luis Borges, Author (1899-1986)
"Of another famous Scandinavian, Charles XII, Voltaire was able to write that he was the most extraordinary person on earth. The superlative mode is an imprudence in that it implies less conviction than mere polemic; but I would apply Voltaire's characterization, not to Charles XII but to that most mysterious of his subjects, Emanuel Swedenborg."

Honoré de Balzac, Author (1799-1850)
"Do you know, I have come back to Swedenborg after vast studies of all religions, and after reading all the works published within the last sixty years? Swedenborg undoubtedly epitomizes all the religions - or rather the one religion - of humanity.

Elizabeth Barret Browning, Poet (1806-1861)
"To my mind the only light that has been cast on the other life is found in Swedenborg's philosophy. It explains much that was incomprehensible."

Thomas Carlyle, Clergyman (1795-1881)
"Swedenborg was a man of great and indisputable cultivation, strong mathematical intellect, and the most pious, seraphic turn of mind; a man beautiful, lovable and tragical to me. More truths are confessed in his writings than in those of any other man. One of the loftiest minds in the realm of mind. One of the spiritual suns that will shine brighter as the years go on."

Walter M. Horton, Professor of Philosophy of Christianity (Oberlin College) (1903-1967)
"In the age of 'one-eyed' reason, as it has been called, Swedenborg was among the very few who kept both eyes open, the eye of the soul and the eye of the senses. By sheer devotion to scientific research he discovered the limitations of science two centuries before Einstein and Eddington; but unlike many prophets of the soul,

he never disparaged reason in the name of faith, or nature in the name of grace. For him, the material and spiritual universes were joined together by multiple correspondences, and an unbroken chain of discrete degrees."

Hiram Powers, American Sculptor (1805-1873)
"Swedenborg is my author. All other writers (in comparison) seem moving in the dark with tapers in hand, groping their way, while he moves in the broad daylight of the sun."

(Edited from the New Church Web site. Accessed 2014: http://www.newchurch.org/about/swedenborg/influence.html)

For more details and references see also:
Writers Influenced By Swedenborg. Web site accessed 2014: http://www.swedenborg.org.uk/emanuel_swedenborg/influences

Jung's Puzzle about Swedenborg

"I admire Swedenborg as a great scientist and a great mystic at the same time. His life and work has always been of great interest to me and I read about seven fat volumes of his writings when I was a medical student." (Jung, *Memories, Dreams, Reflections* (1957)

It remains unclear which Swedenborg books Jung read and how much of them. Searching in Jung's digital version of his *Collected Works* the name Swedenborg is listed 40 times. However when one examines these references most of them are citations in indexes and the remaining few are passing references to Swedenborg's clairvoyant witnessing of a fire in Stockholm that has been well documented and often cited by others. This event is not mentioned in any of Swedenborg's books, but only in personal letters that Swedenborg and others wrote.

The other mention is Jung's reference to Swedenborg's idea of *Homo Maximus* or Grand Man (Human). Nothing else about Swedenborg is cited or referred to in Jung's *Collected Works.* Two possibilities exist about this lack of citation to Swedenborg in Jung's works. One is that Jung as a medical student did not actually read much of Swedenborg's writings, though he was aware of Swedenborg's reputation as a "mystic". And if he did read some of Swedenborg at that early stage in his career, Jung never did it again.

The other explanation as to why Jung does not cite Swedenborg is that Jung was proposing a scientific or empirical approach to the psychological and psychic ideas that he was introducing. Jung was making the claim that his analysis of archetypes, symbols, and religious experiences was not based on subjective visions or mystical experiences that could not be replicated or defined objectively. Citing Swedenborg would have resulted in weakening this claim to objectivity. This explanation has also been proposed in the case of Kant's well known book that criticizes Swedenborg reports.

Here is one of the two citations Jung makes to Swedenborg:

> The doctor in me refuses point blank to consider the life of a people as something that does not conform to psychological law. For him the psyche of a people is only a somewhat more complex structure than the psyche of an individual. Moreover, has not a poet spoken of the "nations of his soul"? And quite correctly, it seems to me, for in one of its aspects the psyche is not individual, but is derived from the nation, from the collectivity, from humanity even. In some way or other we are part of a single, all-embracing psyche, a single "greatest man," the homo maximus to quote Swedenborg. (Jung, *The Spiritual Problem of Modern Man*, p. (176) 2517)

As mentioned, Swedenborg's clairvoyant vision of a fire in his Stockholm home 50 km away, is not mentioned anywhere in his Writings. However the clairvoyant episode is often mentioned by biographers and the letters of those who were witnesses to the event. One reason that Swedenborg was reluctant to publicize his clairvoyant capacities was that miracles, Swedenborg argued, compel spiritual beliefs by persuasion since they are exhibited clearly to the senses. He observed that people whose persuasive faith was based on believing or witnessing miracles in this life, lose this faith when they are resuscitated in the afterlife and their ruling love shoves it to the side and away as something worthless. Hence he avoided mentioning clairvoyant visions that were unrelated to his primary task of presenting the spiritual meaning of *Sacred Scripture*.

Here is a second example of Jung's reference to Swedenborg's so-called clairvoyant event.

> When, for instance, the vision arose in Swedenborg's mind of a fire in Stockholm, there was a real fire raging there at the same time, without there being any demonstrable or even thinkable connection between the two. I certainly would not like to undertake to prove the archetypal connection in this case. I would only point to the fact that in Swedenborg's biography there are certain things which throw a remarkable light on his psychic state. We must assume that there was a lowering of the threshold of consciousness which gave him access to "absolute knowledge." The fire in Stockholm was, in a sense, burning in him too. For the unconscious psyche space and time seem to be relative; that is to say, knowledge finds itself in a space-time continuum in which space is no longer space, nor time. If, therefore, the unconscious should develop or maintain a potential in the direction of consciousness, it is then possible for parallel events to be perceived or known."
> Footnote 15 This case is well authenticated. See report in Kant's Dreams of a Spirit-Seer, Illustrated by Dreams of Metaphysics.
> (Jung, The Archetypes And The Collective Unconscious)

In the history of psychology Jung's intervention in scientific methodology is to be considered critical for the future development of psychology. Jung's influence was to take the field of psychology away from the flattened empiricism that guided its entry into science as an empirical field at around the time early in the twentieth century when Freud and Jung were assuming importance in the fledgling scientific field.

Jung was a profoundly religious person, alive with the living spirit of acknowledgment of the 'other-worldly' and fostering all his life a personal or experiential relationship with God. As is shown in Chapter 3 on Jung's Idea of the Life After Death, he was a deeply religious child and adolescent, strongly tied to the symbols and commandments of spiritual Christianity, though not to its formal organization in society. But when he became a medical "scientist" and practitioner as a young man, and subsequently closely allied to the intellectualism of Freud, Jung embarked with enthusiasm and intensity upon his self-chosen lifelong professional task of creating a *scientific psychology of the spiritual* with which he had been so intensely imbued since childhood, as will be shown further below.

Here is a third citation to Swedenborg in Jung's works. In the following paragraph Jung expresses his striving towards scientific explanations while considering a clairvoyance experience attributed to Swedenborg:

> We are, however, driven to some such assumption if we are not to regress to a magical causality and ascribe to the psyche a power that far exceeds its empirical range of action. In that case we should have to suppose, if we don't want to let causality go, either that Swedenborg's unconscious staged the Stockholm fire, or conversely that the objective event activated in some quite inconceivable manner the corresponding images in Swedenborg's brain. In either case we come up against the unanswerable question of transmission discussed earlier.

> It is of course entirely a matter of subjective opinion which hypothesis is felt to make more sense. Nor does tradition help us much in choosing between magical causality and transcendental meaning, because on the one hand the primitive mentality has always explained synchronicity as magical causality right down to our own day, and on the other hand philosophy assumed a secret correspondence or meaningful connection between natural events until well into the eighteenth century. I prefer the latter hypothesis because it does not, like the first, conflict with the empirical concept of causality, and can count as a principle sui generis. That obliges us, not indeed to correct the principles of natural explanation as hitherto understood, but at least to add to their number, an operation which only the most cogent reasons could justify. I believe, however, that the hints I have given in the foregoing constitute an argument that needs thorough consideration. Psychology, of all the sciences, cannot in the long run afford to overlook such experiences. These things are too important for an understanding of the unconscious, quite apart from their philosophical implications. (Jung, Synchronicity: An Acausal Connecting Principle, p. 481, 483)

Note Jung's reference to the idea of correspondences that marks the central feature of Swedenborg's work: "*philosophy assumed a secret correspondence or meaningful connection between natural events until well into the eighteenth century. I prefer the latter hypothesis because it does not, like the first, conflict with the empirical concept of causality*". Jung is referring to the idea of a cause-effect correspondence between events in the natural world (e.g., a house on fire) and events in the psychic or mental world (e.g., a perception, vision, or premonition).

Jung demonstrates an intense interest in the "Gnostic" writings of spiritually oriented philosophers, as for instance Paracelsus. In the following passage Jung again refers to Swedenborg's idea of the Grand Human or Maximus Homo.

When he [Paracelsus] was thirty-eight, a characteristic change showed itself in his writings: philosophical treatises began to appear alongside his medical ones. "Philosophical" is hardly the right word for this spiritual phenomenon would do better to call it "Gnostic." This remarkable psychic change is one that usually occurs after the midpoint of life has been crossed, and it might be described as a reversal of the psychic current. Only rarely does this subtle change of direction appear clearly on the surface; in most people it takes place, like all the important things in life, beneath the threshold of consciousness. Among those with powerful minds, it manifests itself as a transformation of the intellect into a kind of speculative or intuitive spirituality as for instance in the case of Newton, Swedenborg, and Nietzsche. With Paracelsus, the tension between the opposites was not so marked, though it was noticeable enough.

Everything is contained in it in the form of Plato's "eidola," the archetypes, a germinal idea that may have been implanted in Paracelsus by Marsilio Ficino. The "Limbus" is a circle. The animate world is the larger circle, man is the "Limbus minor," the smaller circle. He is the microcosm. Consequently, everything without is within, everything above is below. Between all things in the larger and smaller circles reigns "correspondence" (correspondentia), a notion that culminates in Swedenborg's homo maximus as a gigantic anthropomorphization of the universe. In the more primitive conception of Paracelsus the anthropomorphization is lacking. (Jung, Paracelsus, p. 7, 13)

Similar movements made themselves felt in the Catholic church, clustering round the strange figure of Johan Joseph von Garres (1776-1848). Especially significant in this respect is his four-volume work Die christliche Mystik (Regensburg, 1836-42). The same trends appear in his earlier book, Emanuel Swedenborg, seine Visionen und sein Verhiiltnis zur Kirche (Speyer, 1827). The Protestant public raved about the soulful poetry of Justinus Kerner and his clairvoyante, Frau Friederike Hauffe, while certain theologians gave vent to their catholicizing tendencies by excommunicating spirits) (Jung, On Spiritualistic Phenomena, p. 701)

Jung's familiarity and involvement with the "spiritualistic" literature is clearly exhibited in his voluminous citations throughout his books and articles, as exemplified in the above quote. Jung was strongly impressed by the report of Swedenborg's clairvoyance and refers to it a dozen times throughout his books. Here is another version of it.

> An excellent example of clairvoyance is preserved for us in philosophical literature and is especially interesting because it was personally commented on by Kant. In an undated letter to Charlotte von Knobloch, he wrote as follows about the spirit-seer Swedenborg: The following occurrence appears to me to have the greatest weight of proof, and to place the assertion respecting Swedenborg's extraordinary gift beyond all possibility of doubt. In the year 1759, towards the end of September, on Saturday at four o'clock p.m., Swedenborg arrived at Gottenburg from England, when Mr. William Castel invited him to his house, together with a party of fifteen persons. About six o'clock Swedenborg went out, and returned to the company quite pale and alarmed. He said that a dangerous fire had just broken out in Stockholm, at the Sodermalm (Gottenburg is about fifty German miles from Stockholm), and that it was spreading very fast. He was restless, and went out often. He said that the house of one of his friends, whom he named, was already in ashes, and that his own was in danger. At eight o'clock, after he had been out again, he joyfully exclaimed, 'Thank God! the fire is extinguished; the third door from my house.' This news occasioned great commotion throughout the whole city, but particularly amongst the company in which he was. It was announced to the Governor the same evening. On Sunday morning Swedenborg was summoned to the Governor who questioned him concerning the disaster.

> Swedenborg described the fire precisely, how it had begun and in what manner it had ceased, and how long it had continued. On the same day the news spread through the city, and as the Governor thought it worthy of attention, the consternation was considerably increased; because many were in trouble on account of their friends and property, which might have been involved in the disaster. On Monday evening a messenger arrived at Gottenburg, who was dispatched by the Board of Trade during the time of the fire. In the letters brought by him, the fire was described precisely in the manner stated by Swedenborg. On Tuesday morning the Royal Courier arrived at the Governor's with the melancholy intelligence of the fire, of the loss which it had occasioned, and of the houses it had

damaged and ruined, not in the least differing from that which Swedenborg had given at the very time when it happened; for the fire was extinguished at eight o'clock.

What can be brought forward against the authenticity of this occurrence (the conflagration in Stockholm)? My friend who wrote this to me has examined all, not only in Stockholm, but also, about two months ago, in Gottenburg, where he is well acquainted with the most respectable houses, and where he could obtain the most authentic and complete information, for as only a very short time had elapsed since 1759, most of the inhabitants are still alive who were eyewitnesses of this occurrence.

Swedenborg, a learned and highly intelligent man, was a visionary of unexampled fertility. His importance is attested by the fact that he had a considerable influence on Kant. (Jung, On Spiritualistic Phenomena, p. 708-714)

Much later in his autobiography dictated just before his passing on, Jung continued to emphasize his lifelong intense interest in "objective psychic phenomena". He seemed to himself to be alone in this attitude and noted the "derision and disbelief" of the people with whom he shared this information.

The observations of the spiritualists, weird and questionable as they seemed to me, were the first accounts I had seen of objective psychic phenomena. Names like Zoellner and Crookes impressed themselves on me, and I read virtually the whole of the literature available to me at the time. Naturally I also spoke of these matters to my comrades, who to my great astonishment reacted with derision and disbelief or with anxious defensiveness. I wondered at the sureness with which they could assert that things like ghosts and table-turning were impossible and therefore fraudulent, and on the other hand at the evidently anxious nature of their defensiveness. I, too, was not certain of the absolute reliability of the reports, but why, after all, should there not be ghosts? How did we know that something was "impossible"? And, above all, what did the anxiety signify? For myself I found such possibilities extremely interesting and attractive. They added another dimension to my life; the world gained depth and background. Could, for example, dreams have anything to do wit ghosts? Kant's Dreams of a Spirit Seer came just at the right moment, and soon I also discovered Karl Duprel, who had evaluated these ideas

> *philosophically and psychologically. I dug up Eschenmayer, Passavant*
> *Justinus Kerner, and Gorres, and read seven volumes of Swedenborg.*
> (Jung, *Memories, Dreams, Reflections*, p. 126)

Jung's persistence was unstoppable. His clear-minded attitude is expressed by his exclamation in the above quote: *"But why, after all, should there not be ghosts? How did we know that something was "impossible"? And, above all, what did the anxiety signify?"* Indeed, Jung found the source of materialism in science, "the anxiety" of scientists when spiritual world topics are raised for examination and study. Jung was facing the negative bias in science against dualism and theism. I myself have felt this in my career of half a century as a scientist and academician. I still feel the pressures of the negative bias now as I remain involved in my career as a psychology professor and researcher. This intellectually and emotionally injurious flattening and crushing attitude towards the human being became the graveyard of modern science as it developed in the twentieth century.

Now however a turnaround in science may be going on. On the professional side, various polls of Western scientists over the past decades indicate that there remains a majority of scientists who believe in the existence of God and of the efficacy of prayer. Interestingly, they do not see this theistic state of mind as a contradiction with the negative bias in science since they hold the view that religion or their faith, and science, are about different things, and there is no conflict felt where there is no overlap. It is clear upon examination of this claim that it is bogus. An omnipotent God is the central active force, hence cause, of every event, natural or spiritual, physical or mental. Swedenborg gives a rational description of this spiritual idea in his analysis of the Laws of Divine Providence.

The central feature of this explanation is that God being infinite, cannot give away any Divine power, which would mean that God would no longer be omnipotent and infinite. Therefore the view of theistic science is that God must be involved and active in every single detail of the natural and spiritual universe. This idea is rationally meaningful because it allows us to see how God can bring about, manage, and create the future in order to bring about God's goals in creating the universe. This goal, as Swedenborg demonstrates, is to maintain a never-ending increase in the population of heaven with human beings from all the earths in the physical universe. The larger the population of heaven, the more perfect it grows, to eternity. The gradual and endless perfection of the human race is thus God's goal in creating and managing the dual universe.

When individuals are ready for passing on, God separates their physical body from the spiritual body by which the person is "resuscitated" in the spiritual world that is also called the world of the afterlife in eternity. The person then enters heaven to eternal marital felicity and blessedness. But if the person's loves and affections are such as to be antagonistic to the loves and attitudes of the people in heaven, they are given a choice between relinquishing those negative loves and accepting the positive heavenly ones, or else, relinquishing all their remaining heavenly loves, and becoming a purely selfish and self-centered personality without any love for others. They then join others in hellish societies that accept and practice such loves on each other. These facts are established by Swedenborg in his careful and repeated ethnographic observations of the afterlife world which he was able to explore with his dual consciousness for 27 continuous years. He wrote three dozen books in which he carefully reported his ethnography of the spiritual world and its societies.

So even today we can justly share Jung's moment of enlightenment and awakening from the illusion of the emperor's new clothes called the scientific method: *"But why, after all, should there not be ghosts? How did we know that something was "impossible"? And, above all, what did the anxiety signify?"* The same anxiety is gripping our generation of scientists today. Their attempt to make a claim that God and science don't overlap is something that gnaws at the edge of their consciousness. It is eating away at their confidence in human rationality. It encourages irrational views in their mind, such as the idea that nature originates and manages the evolution of life. This irrational perspective destroys the rational functioning of the person who believes it and justifies the fabrication by inventive assumptions or spurious facts. And if the rational of the person is impaired, the spiritual cannot be opened and developed, and hence prepared for life in heaven.

As modern minds raised and steeped in science and the scientific method, we must join Jung's initiating battle cry: *"But why, after all, should there not be ghosts?"* We must also be mindful at the same time that not anything people say about ghosts and such ought to be accepted as factual and rational. For the past two and a half centuries the intellectuals, thinkers, and seekers of each generation have found the Writings of Swedenborg directly, or have heard his ideas from others. Hence it could be known to Jung and to us today that there are no ghosts in fact because ghosts are impossible!

What? There are no ghosts?

That's right. No ghosts. Normally ghosts are ascribed to be spirits, or people from the afterlife, who can sometimes be seen with physical eyes as "ghostly" forms. In the work of Swedenborg we can understand rationally why physical eyes cannot see the spiritual world, or why spirits cannot be in physical space or light. The notion of correspondence gives an understanding of discrete degrees or layers of reality, and how God creates and manages the two worlds through the built-in correspondence across the discrete layers. If ghosts don't have a physical body (which everyone loses at death), they are spirits, which means they have a perfectly normal spiritual body. While there is cause-effect correspondence across the two worlds, there is no direct passage or contact possible through the senses. And yet it is the case that if contact by correspondence were interrupted between spirits and us, we would instantly fall into a swoon and expire. But this contact is unconscious for both spirits and us still on earth. More on this will be discussed as we proceed.

So although there indeed are no ghosts yet Jung's awakening was real and could be more justly understood as: *"But why, after all, should there not be spirits, an afterlife, God, and a heaven and hell in eternity?"* This is the true meaning of Jung's awakening cry. And he went on to invent a dual world that includes a psychic world different from the physical world, being a universal collective unconscious that belongs to every human mind from creation, biology, and inheritance. This was totally unlike Freud's idea of a unique and self-contained individual unconscious with every person. After his awakening moment, Jung started using his spiritual-rational level of thinking in order to arrive at rational conclusions that Freud could not accept nor understand with his flattened materialistic cognitions of the unconscious.

As to Jung's puzzle and why he did not cite Swedenborg beyond the two ideas mentioned, it is possible that Jung wanted to avoid a direct connection to Swedenborg given that Jung was at pains in making a claim of scientific empiricism about his discovery of the archetypes and the characterization of the collective unconscious. If this is accurate it explains why Jung was reluctant to cite Swedenborg except on a minimal basis, as explained.

This hypothesis is strengthened by the observation that Jung took up discussion of dozens of esoteric theological concepts that were also discussed at length by Swedenborg. These include:

- the symbolic meaning of the Christian Trinity
- the transcendental elements of the Mass (or Communion, Holy Supper, Eucharist)
- the incarnation and birth of the Eternal Father as God-Man Christ
- the representation of Christ's struggle and death as being also the struggle of every human being in rebirth and regeneration
- the psychological meaning of sacrifice
- the description of correspondences as cause-effect relations between a natural event and a spiritual event

and still other topics that overlap with Swedenborg, some of which will be discussed below. To repeat, none of these topics were referenced to Swedenborg in Jung's extensive work.

When discussing these spiritual topics, Jung cites various Christian Church Fathers and their doctrinal writings from the middle ages. Two possibilities exist. One is that Jung studied Swedenborg but did not wish to acknowledge a direct connection. The other possibility is that Jung did not actually read Swedenborg beyond skimming perhaps, but this would be strange given Jung's lifelong deep interest in spirituality. We therefore fall back on the other hypothesis that citing Swedenborg directly on these topics might hurt Jung's claim that he was investigating religious topics scientifically. At the outset of his monumental work *Psychology and Religion: West and East*, Jung sets up the scientific claim:

> *I approach psychological matters from a scientific and not from a philosophical standpoint. Inasmuch as religion has a very important psychological aspect, I deal with it from a purely empirical point of view, that is, I restrict myself to the observation of phenomena and I eschew any metaphysical or philosophical considerations. I do not deny the validity of these other considerations, but I cannot claim to be competent to apply them correctly. (p. 2)*
>
> ...
>
> *When psychology speaks, for instance, of the motif of the virgin birth,*

it is only concerned with the fact that there is such an idea, but it is not concerned with the question whether such an idea is true or false in any other sense. The idea is psychologically true inasmuch as it exists. Psychological existence is subjective in so far as an idea occurs in only one individual. But it is objective in so far as that idea is shared by a society by a consensus gentium.

This point of view is the same as that of natural science. Psychology deals with ideas and other mental contents as zoology, for instance, deals with the different species of animals. An elephant is "true" because it exists. The elephant is neither an inference nor a statement nor the subjective judgment of a creator. It is a phenomenon. But we are so used to the idea that psychic events are willful and arbitrary products, or even the inventions of a human creator, that we can hardly rid ourselves of the prejudiced view that the psyche and its contents are nothing but our own arbitrary invention or the more or less illusory product of supposition and judgment.

The fact is that certain ideas exist almost everywhere and at all times and can even spontaneously create themselves quite independently of migration and tradition. They are not made by the individual, they just happen to him they even force themselves on his consciousness. This is not Platonic philosophy but empirical psychology. (p. 5)

Had he connected his concepts directly to Swedenborg, Jung could not have continued to claim that his approach was empirical since Swedenborg's "data" were contaminated so to speak, by having been obtained through Swedenborg's visions that are not part of psychological knowledge or understanding. The following comment about Jung's personally revealing book called *The Red Book,* which Jung referred to as "my confrontation with the unconscious", gives additional indication of Jung's anxiety about hurting his reputation as a scientist. It seems that Jung's family heirs shared this view with him and tried at first to prevent the posthumous publication of this book.

Originally, when Jung began to be afflicted by an unceasing flood of apocalyptic visions in 1913, he started to record them in a series of six black journals (subsequently known as the "black books") and later transferred them to the large red leather folio. By 1917, he had finished most of the initial composition of the book but poured over it until 1930, revising, adding commentary, editing (Furlotti).

Despite the technical challenges in mass producing copies of The Red Book that publishers would have faced in Jung's day, Jung did intend for The Red Book to be published. But plans for publication and widespread distribution never reached fruition, in part due to Jung's ambivalence about such a project. Could he expose his own intensely private struggles to a mass audience? Would he be deemed a madman, a mystic, or an unfulfilled artist? Having been ostracized by the psychoanalytic community following his break with Freud (one of the causes of his breakdown), Jung was acutely aware of the risks involved to his reputation. He had said to his close friends on numerous occasions that he wanted to be known first and foremost as a man of science, as a psychologist—an image that might be undermined by the publication of such a fantastic work as The Red Book (Corbett, p. 2).

Jung died in 1961 without having published *The Red Book*. Sensitive to Jung's own misgivings about the risks to his reputation as well as the risks in exposing such extremely personal material, Jung's heirs literally locked the book away in a Swiss bank vault for decades. Despite numerous attempts by hundreds of scholars to see and publish the book, Jung's heirs held to their convictions. Leaks of some of the pages of the manuscript appeared in public, however, and the family eventually relented, concerned that the material might find its way into the hands of Jung's detractors (Corbett, p. 5). It took Jungian scholar and editor Sonu Shamdasani three years of negotiation with Jung's heirs to finally arrange for The Red Book to be published in fall of 2009 (p. 5).

A Beginner's Guide To C.G. Jung's Red Book By Mathew V. Spano. Accessed on the Web in 2015: https://www.quora.com/How-does-one-listen-for-the-Self-in-the-way-that-Carl-Jung-intended-and-discovered-in-the-construction-of-his-The-Red-Book

Dr. Eugene Taylor, a longtime Harvard Professor and writer about spirituality, has noted that Jung's official position in history does not lie in Viennese ties to Freud and to psychoanalysis, but that in actual unrecognized fact Jung is closer to Swedenborg in conceptualizations:

As the details of this interrelation are only now being spelled out, it is possible that Jung's early attraction to the writings of Emanuel Swedenborg, rather than being seen as just some isolated incident, provides yet another clue to the myriad ways that Jungian thought actually has closer affinities to a uniquely English and American rather than Viennese psychology of the subconscious. (Eugene Taylor, *Jung and His Intellectual context: the Swedenborgian Connection.* Web document accessed 2014: http://www.shs.psr.edu/studia/index.asp?article_id=77)

Thus, it is no accident that after his break with Freud, Jung returned periodically to delve into Swedenborg's books. He also read biographies and comments on Swedenborg's life, and he cited Swedenborg on numerous occasions in his own collected works. There are two explanations why this might be so. (Taylor, *Jung and His Intellectual Context*)

Taylor states that Jung "*cited Swedenborg on numerous occasions in his own collected works*". But as I show above these occasions all boil down to only two separate topics, both of which could have come from secondary sources (one of which Jung cites is Gilbert Ballet. *Swedenborg: Histoire d'un visionnaire au XVIII siecle.* Paris, 1899).

Taylor also notes the close connection between Jung and William James to Swedenborg, but this too is a secondary connection not a direct one:

First, the intellectual and spiritual lineage Jung had used to construct a psychology of the unconscious was sympathetic to Swedenborgian thought. William James's father had written some dozen works on Swedenborg, had been instrumental in introducing Swedenborg to the New England transcendentalists, and had evolved a religious philosophy based on the Swedish seer's works that formed the bulwark of the literary legacy inherited by his sons, William and Henry. Then William himself authored almost a dozen more works on psychology and philosophy implicitly answering his father's Swedenborgian metaphysics. Jung, we know, drew particularly from James's -principles of Psychology from his Varieties of Religious Experience, and from his Pragmatism. (Taylor, *Jung and His Intellectual Context*)

Despite the strong background both Jung and William James had indirectly with Swedenborg, it is noteworthy that neither of them cite Swedenborg anywhere in their many volumes, and yet they cite hundreds of other authors. This remains a puzzle to be solved. Taylor further states:

Second, for Jung, Swedenborg's ideas also represented a teleological and mythopoetic iconography of personal transformation. This is most cogently represented in the details of their respective biographies. Both had come from intensely religious families. Both had first turned to science and then ended in religion. Both had made the transition after an extended struggle with the unconscious that led to life transforming experiences. Both evolved a mythic vision of the interior world that had great pragmatic usefulness in their respective careers. Jung thus used Swedenborg in a number of ways to corroborate aspects of his own psychology of the unconscious. (Taylor, Jung and His Intellectual Context)

Taylor's assertion that Jung *"used Swedenborg to corroborate his own psychology of the unconscious"* goes to the heart of Jung's relationship to Swedenborg. Jung did not need to publicly acknowledge this deep relationship to Swedenborg's insights. Their use was personal, individual, and fundamentally relevant to his own regeneration. The drama of Jung's work is his own inner development. Swedenborg's dual consciousness was appropriated as it were by Jung so that he could see into the collective conscious what Swedenborg saw in the spiritual world of the afterlife.

To Jung, Swedenborg's reports were the proof and confirmation of the reality of the collective unconscious and Jung's insight that it contains all of humanity and all that humanity has or can have. Swedenborg's experiences confirmed and proved that the human being is immortal. Jung needed this truth to be a certainty in his mind.

Once Jung received from Swedenborg's work the inner validation for Jung's concept of the collective unconscious, as well as for his experiences of speaking with the departed, Jung thereafter set himself the enormous task of constructing a scientific psychology of the human mind that encompasses and justifies the dynamic relationship between the here and the hereafter. And all along Swedenborg played a stabilizing influence in Jung's mind: "I admire Swedenborg as a great scientist and a great mystic at the same time. His life and work has always been of great interest to me".

Where do people go when they die? Jung was certain now that this is a question of reality that dynamic and analytic psychology must answer, or else it is short and unrealistic. Further, what is the connection between the minds of those who live in the afterlife and those who are on earth? This becomes the fundamental issue for developmental psychology and self-psychology.

Jung often declared that the unconscious is vast, dark, invisible, and even unknowable. Swedenborg on the other hand enjoyed direct observational access to the collective unconscious, which he called the spiritual world that normally becomes conscious only after death. To Swedenborg was given crystal clarity by sight and hearing, but to Jung something shadowy, without form or content, deeply frightening, and unknowable.

Jung's Relationship to Alcoholic Anonymous (AA)

Jung's lifelong involvement with God is confirmed by this exchange of letters between Bill Wilson, Co-founder of AA and C.G. Jung. The letters are exchanged in the year 1961 just a few months before Jung passed into the next life.

First, Bill Wilson's Letter To Dr. Carl Jung , Jan 23, 1961:

> *My dear Dr. Jung:*
> *This letter of great appreciation has been very long overdue.*
> *May I first introduce myself as Bill W., a co-founder of the Society of Alcoholics Anonymous. Though you have surely heard of us, I doubt if you are aware that a certain conversation you once had with one of your patients, a Mr. Rowland H., back in the early 1930's, did play a critical role in the founding of our Fellowship.*
>
> *Though Rowland H. has long since passed away, the recollections of his remarkable experience while under treatment by you has definitely become part of AA history. Our remembrance of Rowland H.'s statements about his experience with you is as follows:*
>
> *Having exhausted other means of recovery from his alcoholism, it was about 1931 that he became your patient. I believe he remained under your*

care for perhaps a year. His admiration for you was boundless, and he left you with a feeling of much confidence.

To his great consternation, he soon relapsed into intoxication. Certain that you were his "court of last resort," he again returned to your care. Then followed the conversation between you that was to become the first link in the chain of events that led to the founding of Alcoholics Anonymous.

My recollection of his account of that conversation is this: First of all, you frankly told him of his hopelessness, so far as any further medical or psychiatric treatment might be concerned. This candid and humble statement of yours was beyond doubt the first foundation stone upon which our Society has since been built.

Coming from you, one he so trusted and admired, the impact upon him was immense. When he then asked you if there was any other hope, you told him that there might be, provided he could become the subject of a spiritual or religious experience - in short, a genuine conversion. You pointed out how such an experience, if brought about, might remotivate him when nothing else could. But you did caution, though, that while such experiences had sometimes brought recovery to alcoholics, they were, nevertheless, comparatively rare. You recommended that he place himself in a religious atmosphere and hope for the best. This I believe was the substance of your advice.

Shortly thereafter, Mr. H. joined the Oxford Groups, an evangelical movement then at the height of its success in Europe, and one with which you are doubtless familiar. You will remember their large emphasis upon the principles of self-survey, confession, restitution, and the giving of oneself in service to others. They strongly stressed meditation and prayer. In these surroundings, Rowland H. did find a conversion experience that released him for the time being from his compulsion to drink.

Returning to New York, he became very active with the "O.G." here, then led by an Episcopal clergyman, Dr. Samuel Shoemaker. Dr. Shoemaker had been one of the founders of that movement, and his was a powerful personality that carried immense sincerity and conviction.

At this time (1932-34) the Oxford Groups had already sobered a number of alcoholics, and Rowland, feeling that he could especially identify with these sufferers, addressed himself to the help of still others. One of these chanced to be an old schoolmate of mine, Edwin T. ("Ebby"). He had been threatened with commitment to an institution, but Mr. H. and another ex-alcoholic "O.G." member procured his parole and helped to bring about his sobriety.

Meanwhile, I had run the course of alcoholism and was threatened with commitment myself. Fortunately I had fallen under the care of a physician - a Dr. William D. Silkworth - who was wonderfully capable of understanding alcoholics. But just as you had given up on Rowland, so had he given me up. It was his theory that alcoholism had two components - an obsession that compelled the sufferer to drink against his will and interest, and some sort of metabolism difficulty which he then called an allergy. The alcoholic's compulsion guaranteed that the alcoholic's drinking would go on, and the allergy made sure that the sufferer would finally deteriorate, go insane, or die. Though I had been one of the few he had thought it possible to help, he was finally obliged to tell me of my hopelessness; I, too, would have to be locked up. To me, this was a shattering blow. Just as Rowland had been made ready for his conversion experience by you, so had my wonderful friend, Dr. Silkworth, prepared me.

Hearing of my plight, my friend Edwin T. came to see me at my home where I was drinking. By then, it was November 1934. I had long marked my friend Edwin for a hopeless case. Yet there he was in a very evident state of "release" which could by no means accounted for by his mere association for a very short time with the Oxford Groups. Yet this obvious state of release, as distinguished from the usual depression, was tremendously convincing. Because he was a kindred sufferer, he could unquestionably communicate with me at great depth. I knew at once I must find an experience like his, or die.

Again I returned to Dr. Silkworth's care where I could be once more sobered and so gain a clearer view of my friend's experience of release, and of Rowland H.'s approach to him.

Clear once more of alcohol, I found myself terribly depressed. This seemed to be caused by my inability to gain the slightest faith. Edwin T. again visited me and repeated the simple Oxford Groups' formulas. Soon after he left me I became even more depressed. In utter despair I cried out, "If there be a God, will He show Himself." There immediately came to me an illumination of enormous impact and dimension, something which I have since tried to describe in the book "Alcoholics Anonymous" and in "AA Comes of Age", basic texts which I am sending you.

My release from the alcohol obsession was immediate. At once I knew I was a free man. Shortly following my experience, my friend Edwin came to the hospital, bringing me a copy of William James' "Varieties of Religious Experience". This book gave me the realization that most conversion experiences, whatever their variety, do have a common denominator of ego collapse at depth. The individual faces an impossible dilemma. In my case the dilemma had been created by my compulsive drinking and the deep feeling of hopelessness had been vastly deepened by my doctor. It was deepened still more by my alcoholic friend when he acquainted me with your verdict of hopelessness respecting Rowland H.

In the wake of my spiritual experience there came a vision of a society of alcoholics, each identifying with and transmitting his experience to the next - chain style. If each sufferer were to carry the news of the scientific hopelessness of alcoholism to each new prospect, he might be able to lay every newcomer wide open to a transforming spiritual experience. This concept proved to be the foundation of such success as Alcoholics Anonymous has since achieved. This has made conversion experiences - nearly every variety reported by James - available on an almost wholesale basis. Our sustained recoveries over the last quarter century number about 300,000. In America and through the world there are today 8,000 AA groups.

So to you, to Dr. Shoemaker of the Oxford Groups, to William James, and to my own physician, Dr. Silkworth, we of AA owe this tremendous benefaction. As you will now clearly see, this astonishing chain of events actually started long ago in your consulting room, and it was directly founded upon your own humility and deep perception.

Very many thoughtful AAs are students of your writings. Because of your conviction that man is something more than intellect, emotion, and two dollars worth of chemicals, you have especially endeared yourself to us.

How our Society grew, developed its Traditions for unity, and structured its functioning will be seen in the texts and pamphlet material that I am sending you.

You will also be interested to learn that in addition to the "spiritual experience," many AAs report a great variety of psychic phenomena, the cumulative weight of which is very considerable. Other members have - following their recovery in AA - been much helped by your practitioners. A few have been intrigued by the "I Ching" and your remarkable introduction to that work.

Please be certain that your place in the affection, and in the history of the Fellowship, is like no other.

Gratefully yours,
William G. W.
Co-founder Alcoholics Anonymous

Now here is Jung's answer, written almost immediately: (accessed on the Web in 2015: http://www.barefootsworld.net/jungletter.html)

PROF. DR. C. G. JUNG

KÜSNACHT-ZÜRICH
SEESTRASSE 228

January 30, 1961

Mr. William G. Wilson
Alcoholics Anonymous
Box 459 Grand Central Station
New York 17, N.Y.

Dear Mr. Wilson,

your letter has been very welcome indeed.

I had no news from Roland H. anymore and often wondered what has been his fate.
Our conversation which he has adequately reported to you had an aspect of which
he did not know. The reason was, that I could not tell him everything, was that
those days I had to be exceedingly careful of what I said. I had found out that
I was misunderstood in every possible way. Thus I was very careful when I talked
to Roland H. But what I really thought about, was the result of many experiences
with men of his kind.

His craving for alcohol was the equivalent on a low level of the spiritual
thirst of our being for wholeness, expressed in mediaeval language: the union
with God. [1)]

How could one formulate such an insight in a language that is not misunderstood
in our days?

The only right and legitimate way to such an experience is, that it happens to
you in reality and it can only happen to you when you walk on a path, which leads
you to higher understanding. You might be led to that goal by an act of grace
or through a personal and honest contact with friends, or through a higher
education of the mind beyond the confines of mere rationalism. I see from your
letter that Roland H. has chosen the second way, which was, under the circumstances, obviously the best one.

I am strongly convinced that the evil principle prevailing in this world, leads
the unrecognized spiritual need into perdition, if it is not counteracted either
by a real religious insight or by the protective wall of human community. An
ordinary man, not protected by an action from above and isolated in society
cannot resist the power of evil, which is called very aptly the Devil. But the
use of such words arouse so many mistakes that one can only keep aloof from
them as much as possible.

These are the reasons why I could not give a full and sufficient explanation to
Roland H. but I am risking it with you, because I conclude from your very
decent and honest letter, that you have acquired a point of view above the mis-
leading platitudes, one usually hears about alcoholism.

You see, Alcohol in Latin is "spiritus" and you use the same word for the
highest religious experience as well as for the most depraving poison. The helpful formula therefore is: spiritus contra spiritum.

Thanking you again for your kind letter

I remain

                    yours sincerely   C. G. Jung.

[1)] "As the hart panteth after the water brooks, so
   panteth my soul after thee, O God." (Psalm 42,1)

It is known that the success of AA in rehabilitating "hopeless" alcoholics is closely involved with each member becoming convinced that they are helpless in changing themselves but that God can do it when you give yourself and your life over to Him.

In Bill Wilson's letter to Jung he refers to a conversation that Jung had 30 years before with one of his patients who was an alcoholic: "that conversation between you was to become the first link in the chain of events that led to the founding of Alcoholics Anonymous". Wilson specifies: "My recollection of his account of that conversation is this: First of all, you frankly told him of his hopelessness, so far as any further medical or psychiatric treatment might be concerned. ... When he then asked you if there was any other hope, you told him that there might be, provided he could become the subject of a spiritual or religious experience - in short, a genuine conversion. You pointed out how such an experience, if brought about, might remotivate him when nothing else could."

Jung confirms in his answer to Wilson that the conversation was "adequately reported" by his patient. We can conclude from this that Jung was a deeply religious man, that he had undergone religious conversion, and that he obtained motivation or strength fro his personal relationship to God. These elements are discussed as well in other sections of this Chapter. At the same time Jung's letter reveals his lifelong preoccupation with keeping his relationship to God from appearing openly in his practice, lectures, and writings. He was focused on the work of constructing psychological knowledge that is scientific, and this cannot be based on personal experience, either his own or that of a visionary or mystic. He had to be careful not to have his psychiatric practice be based on religion or his own religious conversion.

About that conversation with his alcoholic patient Jung tells Bill Wilson that "I could not tell him everything...In those days I had to be exceedingly careful of what I said." Jung reveals what he thought of that he could not say to his patient for fear of being misunderstood or misreported. It was this: "His craving for alcohol was the equivalent of ... the spiritual thirst of our being for wholeness, expressed ... as the union with God." And he quotes from Psalm 42:1 in the Old Testament of the Bible: "As the heart panteth after the water brooks, so panteth my soul after thee, O God". Jung commiserates: "How could one formulate such an insight in a language that Is not misunderstood in our days?"

36

Jung shares his conviction that "the evil principle prevailing in this world leads the unrecognized spiritual need into perdition, if it is not counteracted by a real religious insight". Jung saw "real religious insight" as involving a personal and meaningful relationship with God. He warns that "an ordinary man not protected by an action from above ... cannot resist the power of evil, which is called very aptly the Devil." Jung states that "these are the reasons why I could not give a full and sufficient explanation to Roland H. but I am risking it with you".

It is noteworthy that Jung ends his letter to Bill Wilson with this statement:

> "Alcohol in Latin is "spiritus" and you use the same word for the highest religious experience as well as for the most depraving poison. The helpful formula therefore is: spiritus contra spiritum."

This title in Latin encapsulates Jung's religiosity and dualism. He is acknowledging thereby the existence of spiritual good and evil that are powerfully active in the mind of individuals. God's angelic forces of good ("spiritus") battle the devil's infernal forces of evil. As it is made clear in the Writings of Swedenborg, the human mind is a battleground between societies of good spirits and hoards of evil spirits. Mental alcoholism is a spiritual disease caused by evil psychic forces in the collective unconscious.

Bill Wilson, in his account to Jung, tells his own desperate story of being unable to rid himself of the alcoholism that was killing him. But in the end he won: "In utter despair I cried out, "If there be a God, will He show Himself." There immediately came to me an illumination of enormous impact and dimension, something which I have since tried to describe in the book "Alcoholics Anonymous" and in "AA Comes of Age", basic texts which I am sending you. My release from the alcohol obsession was immediate. At once I knew I was a free man."

The first three steps of the 12 step program are the most critical, which is why they are placed in rank 1, 2, and 3. Nothing can succeed in the other steps without these first three. And the tragic long painful failure of the alcoholic man and woman will continue if the first two steps are not completed. The first step is to declare psychological bankruptcy or failure. This must come after years of seeing one's life break apart at the seams despite our desperate attempts to control our mental sickness. We must admit defeat. We must see that we are completely hopeless trying to solve our problem by ourselves. That is step 1. Nothing goes without it. To admit hopelessness, and to actually mean it, is to give up arrogance and self-pride. Now there is room for step 2.

Step 2 is to replace the self that is at the helm of our mind with God instead being at the helm. This is the confession and admission of the existence of a "Higher Power", higher than one's own power. The quote below from the official AA guidebook shows up various types of mental conflicts that new AA members have regularly experienced in the form of rebelling against faith, invocation, and reliance on God. Nearly everyone has a culture of religion from childhood but many have in their adult life departed from that "childish" idea and idea of God. This constitutes an intellectual rejection of God. Others experience an emotional rejection because God wouldn't do what they asked Him for, or worse, God did not protect their loved ones from disaster and early death.

But all this psychological resistance is just that, resistance. It does not present an actual obstacle that prevents the solution. With practice and group support the new members gain courage in dethroning themselves from their delusional status, and this action allows God in.

Quoting from the *Second Step* of the AA *12 Step Program* (accessed on the Web in 2015 at: http://www.aa.org/assets/en_US/en_step2.pdf)

> As psychiatrists have often observed, defiance is the outstanding characteristic of many an alcoholic. So it's not strange that lots of us have had our day at defying God Himself. Sometimes it's because God has not delivered us the good things of life which we specified, as a greedy child makes an impossible list for Santa Claus. More often, though, we had met up with some major calamity, and to our way of thinking lost out because God deserted us. The girl we wanted to marry had other notions; we prayed God that she'd change her mind, but she didn't. We prayed for healthy children, and were presented with sick ones, or none at all. We prayed for promotions at business, and none came. Loved ones, upon whom we heartily depended, were taken from us by so-called acts of God. Then we became drunkards, and asked God to stop that. But nothing happened. This was the unkindest cut of all. 'Damn this faith business!' we said.

"When we encountered A.A., the fallacy of our defiance was revealed. At no time had we asked what God's will was for us; instead we had been telling Him what it ought to be. No man, we saw, could believe in God and defy Him, too. Belief meant reliance, not defiance. In A.A. we saw the fruits of this belief: men and women spared from alcohol's final catastrophe. We saw them meet and transcend their other pains and trials. We saw them calmly accept impossible situations, seeking neither to run nor to recriminate. This was not only faith; it was faith that worked under all conditions. We soon concluded that whatever price in humility we must pay, we would pay."

The AA Guide points to the ineffectiveness of traditional religious interventions with alcoholics. These have no power over the sickness. In contrast to this, a personal relationship with God does have the power to heal the mental sickness of the alcoholic victim.

To clergymen, doctors, friends, and families, the alcoholic who means well and tries hard is a heartbreaking riddle. To most A.A.'s, he is not. There are too many of us who have been just like him, and have found the riddle's answer. This answer has to do with the quality of faith rather than its quantity. This has been our blind spot. We supposed we had humility when really we hadn't. We supposed we had been serious about religious practices when, upon honest appraisal, we found we had been only superficial. Or, going to the other extreme, we had wallowed in emotionalism and had mistaken it for true religious feeling. In both cases, we had been asking something for nothing. The fact was we really hadn't cleaned house so that the grace of God could enter us and expel the obsession. In no deep or meaningful sense had we ever taken stock of ourselves, made amends to those we had harmed, or freely given to any other human being without any demand for reward. We had not even prayed rightly. We had always said, "Grant me my wishes" instead of "Thy will be done." The love of God and man we understood not at all. Therefore we remained self-deceived, and so incapable of receiving enough grace to restore us to sanity.

Therefore, Step Two is the rallying point for all of us. Whether agnostic, atheist, or former believer, we can stand together on this Step. True humility and an open mind can lead us to faith, and every A.A. meeting is an assurance that God will restore us to sanity if we rightly relate ourselves to Him.

Jung's precocious genius also saw into the hypocritical worship and religion of his parents and boyhood culture, and hated it. Like Freud he could have become an atheist who ridiculed people who believed in God. Instead, Jung initiated his own personal relationship with God and throughout his long life he relied on that relationship from which he drew the strength to be a radical innovator.

Swedenborg describes faith as growing through two phases of development. First in the external phase, we believe that salvation is from our faith and the strength of our self-confidence as being justified by that faith. This is a superficial state that does not penetrate into the interior levels of our personality where our inmost loves reside. These loves are selfish and primitive. In the afterlife the superficial faith is cast off as the inmost loves emerge to the surface. These loves care nothing for mutual love or respect, and are focused exclusively on gaining dominance over everyone else for the sake of self-gain and self-supremacy.

But those who leave this phase behind and enter the "inner chamber" of a sincere relationship with God, are confronted and challenged whenever the selfish love dictates some thought, word, or action. The power of God confronts the selfish love and challenges it to a duel. The person experiences this spiritual battle as a temptation to act contrary to faith and principle for the sake of satisfying some selfish love. This is the level of battle that the alcoholic faces. The entire hells are on one side holding the person in captivity through the attachment to alcohol; and the angels are on the other side of the person giving strength and determination to hold on to principle and promise.

Managing the evil psychic forces that incite the obsession for alcohol is possible when you get to know these forces and where they get their strength. The AA program makes it a central feature of recovery the condition of thinking of others before you think of yourself. The obsession for alcohol is held in place by selfishness and considering self before everyone else. Therefore the cure from that obsession is the elimination of selfishness and the initiation of mutual love, altruism, love of God, desire to be useful to others, being kind and considerate, repenting, making restitution, offering services.

This approach is fully compatible with the psychology of Jung and Swedenborg. In fact they both offer involved explanations of how the process works. Jung calls it "individuation or self-realization", while Swedenborg calls it "regeneration". The process involves knowing self and being true to self – but not to selfishness, which is inherited and is not one's true self. Swedenborg was able to see the appearance of the self, which he called the "proprium of man" from the Latin word meaning "one's own". He testifies that the Fallen human proprium has a monstrous and deformed appearance and almost devoid of anything belonging to human life which is intelligent and social. This is the self of destruction. It is called the devil.

The alcoholic has many things in common to other human behavior that is depraved and injurious to self and community. All such destructive and negative behavior gets attached to the victim or patient who has abandoned the principle that in everything we do that affects others we are to consider their welfare and comfort equally with our own. The alcoholic, the gambler, or the cheat does not do this.

Continuing with Step 3: Affirmative Action

> "Made a decision to turn our will and our lives over to the care of God as we understood Him."

PRACTICING Step Three is like the opening of a door which to all appearances is still closed and locked. All we need is a key, and the decision to swing the door open. There is only one key, and it is called willingness. Once unlocked by willingness, the door opens almost of itself, and looking through it, we shall see a pathway beside which is an inscription. It reads: "This is the way to a faith that works." In the first two Steps we were engaged in reflection. We saw that we were powerless over alcohol, but we also perceived that faith of some kind, if only in A.A. itself, is possible to anyone. These conclusions did not require action; they required only acceptance.

Like all the remaining Steps, Step Three calls for affirmative action, for it is only by action that we can cut away the self-will which has always blocked the entry of God—or, if you like, a Higher Power—into our lives. Faith, to be sure, is necessary, but faith alone can avail nothing. We can have faith, yet keep God out of our lives. Therefore our problem now becomes just how and by what specific
means shall we be able to let Him in? Step Three represents our first attempt to do this. In fact, the effectiveness of the whole A.A. program will rest upon

how well and earnestly we have tried to come to "a decision to turn our will and our lives over to the care of God as we understood Him"

Of critical importance is to understand the idea that "These conclusions did not require action; they required only acceptance". It is not enough to accept God, to accept faith, to accept the Ten Commandments, or to accept that there is heaven and hell. Acceptance is a necessary but insufficient condition for salvation. There is no life or power in acceptance, consequently there is no change of personality from self-directed habits to other-directed. Everyone knows the saying that "action speaks louder than words". "Affirmative action" means that the individual is struggling to act and think in accordance with one's faith, or understanding of the doctrine of one's faith.

A faith must lead to doctrine and this to action and performance according to doctrine. The first requirement for affirmative action is to stop the objectionable behavior, thoughts, and habits. Doctrine defines what is objectionable. This requires struggling to overcome temptations and doubts. This is the struggle and effort into which God's power enters and makes change possible.

The empowering of the will is not by faith but by the struggle to resist one's old self.

Continuing with Step 3 of A.A.:

> But suppose that instinct still cries out, as it certainly will, *"Yes, respecting alcohol, I guess I have to be dependent upon A.A., but in all other matters I must still maintain my independence. Nothing is going to turn me into a nonentity. If I keep on turning my life and my will over to the care of Something or Somebody else, what will become of me? I'll look like the hole in the doughnut."*

> This, of course, is the process by which instinct and logic always seek to bolster egotism, and so frustrate spiritual development. The trouble is that this kind of thinking takes no real account of the facts. And the facts seem to be these:

> The more we become willing to depend upon a Higher Power, the more independent we actually are. Therefore dependence, as A.A. practices it, is really a means of gaining true independence of the spirit.

42

"The facts" are fully confirmed by Swedenborg who interviewed many inhabitants already in the afterlife and existing in the upper regions of the mental world called the heavenly communities. Swedenborg calls them "angels" and they live as married couples in conjugial love and in mutual love with their neighbors, and in love to God with whom they have a close relationship. All the angels reported that they feel most happy, most free, and most like their true self when their proprium-self is shut down and remains uninvolved and a distance. The moment they feel the desire to arouse their proprium and to assert themselves as they were before, they instantly sink in consciousness to a lower level that is no longer their heaven. This happens seldom and only with some of them who appear unable to completely abandon their own proprium once and for all.

People in the afterlife can "enter their heaven" whenever they desire other people's welfare and comfort before their own. If they can be happy that way then they can be in the mental atmospheres of heaven. In the afterlife no one can settle into any mental zone except that which is in accord with their ruling love or deepest love, which is the love that commands all other loves and has its way with them. These facts hold true in this life as well. When we are in natural consciousness our faith is self-serving and we take meritorious refuge in our outward acts of religion and faith, hoping they will save us despite our attraction to and continued practice of evil things that prevent our personality change, and consequently prevent our salvation.

Continuing with Step 4 of AA: Reigning in Our Instincts

Made a searching and fearless moral inventory of ourselves.

CREATION gave us instincts for a purpose. Without them we wouldn't be complete human beings. If men and women didn't exert themselves to be secure in their persons, made no effort to harvest food or construct shelter, there would be no survival. If they didn't reproduce, the earth wouldn't be populated. If there were no social instinct, if men cared nothing for the society of one another, there would be no society. So these desires—for the sex relation, for material and emotional security, and for companionship—are perfectly necessary and right, and surely God-given.

Yet these instincts, so necessary for our existence, often far exceed their proper functions. Powerfully, blindly, many times subtly, they drive us, dominate us, and insist upon ruling our lives. Our desires for sex, for material and emotional security, and for an important place in society often tyrannize us. When thus out of joint, man's natural desires cause him great trouble, practically all the trouble there is. No human being, however good, is exempt from these troubles. Nearly every serious emotional problem can be seen as a case of misdirected instinct. When that happens, our great natural assets, the instincts, have turned into physical and mental liabilities.

We want to find exactly how, when, and where our natural desires have warped us. We wish to look squarely at the unhappiness this has caused others and ourselves. By discovering what our emotional deformities are, we can move toward their correction. Without a willing and persistent effort to do this, there can be little sobriety or contentment for us. Without a searching and fearless moral inventory, most of us have found that the faith which really works in daily living is still out of reach.

To practice being good is the secret to overcoming alcoholism and all other weaknesses and mental dysfunctions. "Being good" means acting in accordance with one's moral principles, while flouting or breaking them is "being bad". Character weakness is initiated and maintained by being bad in this sense. We put our life in the hands of God when we are being good. The pride of self-intelligence and the desire to dominate others for one's benefit is to be bad, and it leads to a downward spiral to the hells that live in our mind. Jung frequently warned that to ignore the psychic forces is to become their victim. There are benign and helpful psychic forces and there are dark and harmful forces that delight in bringing suffering upon those who are unprepared to resist them. Alcoholism and other mental sicknesses are the consequences of the 'wages of sin', the chief of which is lack of humility and arrogance. When the mind banishes humility, the self becomes god, or more accurately, devil-god. This is the inborn instinct of loving self for the sake of self and favoring others only so long as they favor us and are willing to serve us.

Continuing with Step 4 of AA on the restoration of morality and spiritual sanity:

Every time a person imposes his instincts unreasonably upon others, unhappiness follows. If the pursuit of wealth tramples upon people who happen to be in the way, then anger, jealousy, and revenge are likely to be aroused. If sex runs riot, there is a similar uproar. Demands made upon other people for too much attention, protection, and love can only invite domination or revulsion in the protectors themselves—two emotions quite as unhealthy as the demands which evoked them. When an individual's desire for prestige becomes uncontrollable, whether in the sewing circle or at the international conference table, other people suffer and often revolt. This collision of instincts can produce anything from a cold snub to a blazing revolution. In these ways we are set in conflict not only with ourselves, but with other people who have instincts, too.

If temperamentally we are on the depressive side, we are apt to be swamped with guilt and self-loathing. We wallow in this messy bog, often getting a misshapen and painful pleasure out of it. As we morbidly pursue this melancholy activity, we may sink to such a point of despair that nothing but oblivion looks possible as a solution. Here, of course, we have lost all perspective, and therefore all genuine humility. For this is pride in reverse. This is not a moral inventory at all; it is the very process by which the depressive has so often been led to the bottle and extinction.

If, however, our natural disposition is inclined to self-righteousness or grandiosity, our reaction will be just the opposite. We will be offended at A.A.'s suggested inventory. No doubt we shall point with pride to the good lives we thought we led before the bottle cut us down. We shall claim that our serious character defects, if we think we have any at all, have been caused chiefly by excessive drinking. This being so, we think it logically follows that sobriety— first, last, and all the time—is the only thing we need to work for. We believe that our one-time good characters will be revived the moment we quit alcohol. If we were pretty nice people all along, except for our drinking, what need is there for a moral inventory now that we are sober?

Making a moral inventory is the process of knowing oneself by observing and monitoring our thoughts, attitudes, reactions, and actions. One of the principal villains in our unreformed personality is the feeling of meritoriousness while justifying ourselves as basically being a good person, with some mistakes here and there. This is the face of hypocrisy, the veil of perdition. It is the rejection of God and the surrender to the devil. It quickly and steadily degenerates into character weakness, suffering, and hell. The opposite is needed, namely, to convict ourselves as corrupt through and through and beyond repair. Thus, hopelessness. Then the reversal or conversion. Self is corrupt and hopeless and inimical. We have found the enemy within: it is the self.

The sponsors of those who feel they need no inventory are confronted with quite another problem. This is because people who are driven by pride of self unconsciously blind themselves to their liabilities. These newcomers scarcely need comforting. The problem is to help them discover a chink in the walls their ego has built, through which the light of reason can shine.

But in A.A. we slowly learned that something had to be done about our vengeful resentments, self-pity, and unwarranted pride. We had to see that every time we played the big shot, we turned people against us. We had to see that when we harbored grudges and planned revenge for such defeats, we were really beating ourselves with the club of anger we had intended to use on others. We learned that if we were seriously disturbed, our first need was to quiet that disturbance, regardless of who or what we thought caused it.

Now let's ponder the need for a list of the more glaring personality defects all of us have in varying degrees. To those having religious training, such a list would set forth serious violations of moral principles. Some others will think of this list as defects of character. Still others will call it an index of maladjustments. Some will become quite annoyed if there is talk about immorality, let alone sin. But all who are in the least reasonable will agree upon one point: that there is plenty wrong with us alcoholics about which plenty will have to be done if we are to expect sobriety, progress, and any real ability to cope with life.

But the testimony of A.A.'s who have really tried a moral inventory is that pride and fear of this sort turn out to be bogeymen, nothing else. Once we have a complete willingness to take inventory, and exert ourselves to do the job thoroughly, a wonderful light falls upon this foggy scene. As we persist, a brand-new kind of confidence is born, and the sense of relief at finally facing ourselves is indescribable. These are the first fruits of Step Four.

It is interesting to note that both Jung and Swedenborg exerted an influence in the establishment and application of the Alcoholic Anonymous program that has been acknowledged worldwide as having spectacular and even miraculous effectiveness. Both Jung and Swedenborg argued that the individual psyche is powerless to contain the injurious forces that surrounds the spirit of every person. The alcoholic, the drug addict, the psychopath, and the self-centered person all have this in common that they are under the influence and power of these hostile psychic forces in the collective unconscious. Jung said that few of his patients ever got really better except those who were able to awaken in themselves a religious feeling of dependence on God. Jung also observed that his older patients were more receptive to the idea of life after death as they saw themselves approach closer to that phase of life's apparent ending.

The relationship between Swedenborg's spiritual ideas and the 12 Step Program of Alcoholics Anonymous is described on a Web site:

> AA was co-founded in 1935 by Bill Wilson and Dr. Bob Smith. Bill Wilson first came into contact with Swedenborg's writings in the summer of 1915 while falling in love with Lois Burnham. Lois was the granddaughter of the Rev. N.C. Burnham, a Swedenborgian scholar and one of the founders of the Swedenborgian Academy of the New Church in Pennsylvania. Her family was very active in the New Church, and in 1918 Bill and Lois were married in the Swedenborgian church in Brooklyn, New York. After the worst part of Bill's battle with alcoholism and his founding of AA, Lois founded the companion group Al-Anon for support to family and close friends of those afflicted with the disease of alcoholism. Her activities with Al-Anon and her references to her Swedenborgian background are detailed in her autobiography, Lois Remembers.
>
> True to his mission in developing AA as a non-sectarian path to help alcoholics fight their disease, Bill Wilson never mentioned Swedenborg's Writings as a source for his Twelve Steps. However, just as clear is the complete harmony between Swedenborg's teachings on spiritual growth and development and the fundamental principles of the Twelve Steps. AA's Twelve Steps make a wonderful outline of Swedenborg's teachings on the process of repentance, reformation and regeneration.
>
> Twelve-step programs have been a tremendous help to many people, both for those trying to break free from an addition and for their families. The various twelve-step groups all have their foundation in the twelve steps of AA as they are spelled out in the book Alcoholics Anonymous, by Bill Wilson.
>
> Twelve Steps of Alcoholics Anonymous

We admitted we were powerless over alcohol-that our lives had become unmanageable.

Came to believe that a Power greater than ourselves could restore us to sanity.

Made a decision to turn our will and our lives over to the care of God as we understood Him.

Made a searching and fearless moral inventory of ourselves.
Admitted to God, to ourselves, and to another human being the exact nature of our wrongs.

Were entirely ready to have God remove all these defects of character. Humbly asked Him to remove our shortcomings.

Made a list of all persons we had harmed, and became willing to make amends to them all.

Made direct amends to such people wherever possible, except when to do so would injure to them all.

Continued to take personal inventory and when we were wrong, promptly admitted it.

Sought through prayer and meditation to improve our conscious contact with God as we understood Him, praying only for knowledge of His will for us and the power to carry that out.

Having had a spiritual awakening as the result of these steps, we tried to carry this message to alcoholics and to practice these principles in all our affairs.
http://www.oakarbor.org/why_oakarbor/wilsons.html

The acknowledgment of one's powerlessness to fight addiction and pathology is the beginning of spiritual insight.

In the mental state of spiritual consciousness people perceive what they cannot perceive in natural consciousness, namely, that *only God has power to heal and set straight.*

In natural consciousness we cannot acknowledge this reality and we deny it. We are persuaded by our senses that tell us that we act and think from ourselves not from someone else. Hence if we think right and solve some problem we attribute the efficacy and knowledge to ourselves, of our experience and intelligence. This is the trap of natural consciousness. There is only what the senses can detect directly, or with instruments and measurements. There is no other reality. Mind is an illusion that ceases with the death of the body. God is a personal, subjective and psychological belief. It is not a scientific fact. Life after death is an improbable idea. Heaven and hell are for children stories. Etc. This is the materialistic mind that we develop from our socialization, education, and sensual experience.

All we need to do to defeat this delusion is to find a chink in its armor and destroy the illusion and persuasion. This weakness in the armor is found when we take the big step, the jump. We acknowledge that *only God has power to heal and set straight.* By ourselves we can do nothing. All along what we did was not from ourselves but from God through others.

When this acknowledgment becomes an intellectual belief and an inner certainty, spiritual consciousness immediately kicks in. The person is now enlightened. And therefore saved!

The individual is to acknowledge and accept God's help in order to obtain it. Swedenborg experienced in full consciousness and perception the fury and naked savagery of the evil psychic forces that assail the spirit of every individual. He described how the entire hells of numberless devils and demons are involved in every attack upon a single person. *It is impossible to resist them.* The devils also believe that they are attacking from themselves and from their own power, not knowing or acknowledging that they have no power whatsoever on their own but are able to do this from God's power that is *acting through them and directing them to God's goals,* which is that the individual may be saved and live happy in heaven forever.

Without allowing some attacks from the evil psychic forces no individual could be regenerated and saved for heaven. These psychic attacks are employed by God to place the individual into a mental state of suffering, fear, and temptation. Without spiritual temptation no one can be reformed because it is necessary for the person to reject their own evil by facing it and in total freedom without coercion to reject it and to choose good, invoking God's help and mercy. This procedure is efficacious over and over again until all the major evils of the individual are faced, rejected, and not done. When an evil in oneself is seen and rejected and not done, the opposite to that evil then is implanted by God and it grows into new regenerated abilities of doing good by avoiding doing evil.

In order to manage all the details of the universe God acts through both the good or well disposed and the evil or hateful. Since the Fall, all human beings on this earth have been born with anatomical ties to both the good in heaven and the evil in hell. God uses both the good and the evil to act and bring about conditions around us that excite our various emotions and thoughts. God allows evil spirits to tempt the alcoholic by exciting and intensifying the desire for a drink, and at the same time weakening the alcoholic's resolution not to drink and infusing all sorts of thoughts that justify making an exception on this occasion.

While allowing this attack by the evil spirits, God brings good spirits into communication with the alcoholic and they act to strengthen the person's resolve not to take that drink and not to make an exception. This is the battle that gives the alcoholic the opportunity to strengthen his character and confidence in overcoming and being successful. Without this interior spiritual battle the alcoholic cannot reform. Only in this spiritual battle, where the evil and good forces are balanced, can the person choose the good while being in a state of spiritual freedom. Whatever we choose in freedom is from love and remains as part of our personality structure forever.

Swedenborg's Special Status

For the past two and a half centuries the writings of Emanuel Swedenborg (1688-1772) have been a persistent and continuous topic in the literature of religion, spirituality, theology, psychology, neuroanatomy, biology, and physics. Specific citations will be found throughout the article. Unlike other well-known writers of the seventeenth and eighteenth centuries such as Leibnitz, Descartes, Oetinger, and Kant, the new concepts that Swedenborg was introducing were presented as based on his direct exploration of the transcendent realm, or as he called it the "spiritual world". Furthermore, Swedenborg's work contrasts with the others in his use of the Bible as an exclusive and absolute source of confirmation for all spiritual knowledge. In addition to Scriptural confirmation Swedenborg provides many ethnographic eyewitness reports of the life, manners, language, philosophical ideas and religious beliefs held by those who passed on through death from the natural world into the spiritual world of the afterlife, which he placed apart from time" and "in eternity".

Swedenborg not only reports hitherto unheard of details about the afterlife but also anchors these details specifically to the text of the Old and New Testaments *when the verses are understood spiritually* rather than simply naturally and historically. He therefore had to demonstrate the unique method of exegesis that he created based on the idea of "correspondences". His method of derivation or extraction of the interior spiritual meaning from the outer literal sense of the text is explained in this article.

Reactions to these two unique and striking aspects of Swedenborg's method and system of religious thought have been controversial. Even in his time this rejection and hostility was exhibited by the Swedish Lutheran State Church who put his early publications on a heresy trial as being inconsistent with Christian doctrine and his early books were temporarily banished. Later however this decision was reversed by the King, and Swedenborg continued to publish outside Sweden more than two-dozen books on his new ideas about Christianity. (1) One of Swedenborg's books that came to the attention of Church authorities in Germany ("probably arranged") was confiscated and banished as "an offense against religion and theology". (2)

   Note: The numbers in parentheses throughout this Section refer to reference notes that appear at the end of the Section.

Swedenborg is the only reputed scientist in modern science history to have claimed to have dual consciousness continuously for the last 27 years of his life. The expression "dual consciousness" is introduced here to refer to *fully awake mental functioning simultaneously in the natural mind and in the spiritual mind.* Swedenborg described the transition of a person at death from consciousness in the natural mind to consciousness in the spiritual mind. He reports from direct observation that with the death of the physical body people no longer have awareness of the physical world. Instead they live fully conscious lives in the spiritual world of the afterlife (which will be discussed below). Swedenborg, unlike the normal pattern, became fully conscious simultaneously in both worlds for nearly three decades before his death. He wrote more than two-dozen books and extensive ethnographies reporting in detail on his experiences as a dual consciousness person. This article examines his substantive theory of consciousness and shows its relation to the dual universe and their contents.

Swedenborg had a distinguished career in Sweden as a mining engineer, publisher of scientific works, and respected member of the Swedish Housel of Lords. (3) By the time he was 57 years old Swedenborg had published innovative and serious scientific works in physics, chemistry, psychology, anatomy, and physiology, besides some early contributions in metallurgy, crystallography, and mechanics. He designed a "flying machine" in 1743. (4) A model of it was reproduced in the *National Air and Space Museum*. Swedenborg was a keen observer, being the first to conclude from the data of anatomists of his day that the cerebrum and left brain deal with the intellect and reasoning (cognitive functions), while the cerebellum and right brain deal with the will and motivation (affective system). He also made other neuroanatomical observations that anticipate the much later discovery of the neuron and the cerebrospinal fluid. (5)

Swedenborg's works in the natural and anatomical sciences stood in contrast with other scientific works of his day in that he tries to trace all scientific phenomena and principles to the spiritual realm and ultimately to "God, the Creator" as the First Cause. He described the natural world as the "world of effects" and the spiritual world as the "world of causes". Every single natural event is an effect of a prior spiritual event, which is the cause of it. Swedenborg's view of science is that the apparent cause-effect relations observable in the physical plane are actually to be defined as correlations. Only by studying the phenomena of both worlds *together* – spiritual cause and natural effect, can reality be scientifically understood. Further, all causes in the universe originate from one source, which Swedenborg identifies as "God the that exist and is their First Cause. Swedenborg's system is therefore within the philosophical tradition known as "theistic" and "dualist". (6)

Swedenborg had to learn how to function with dual consciousness, going about his busy daily schedule as a mining engineer and science publisher, and at the same time walking around and conversing with the "departed" already in the afterlife of the spiritual world of eternity. Evidence that human beings live in the afterlife is given by the report of Swedenborg's conversations with many individuals known to him only from history (e.g., Aristotle, some of the disciples of Jesus, Newton, and many others). He also had numerous and repeated conversations in the spiritual world with those with whom he had been personally acquainted in Sweden prior to their death These extraordinary supernatural claims were not well received by many (7), yet Swedenborg has had a consistent following worldwide for the past 250 years. (8)

Swedenborg's writings consist of some 30 published volumes in Latin giving theoretical explanations and empirical descriptions of the human mind as it appears objectively from within and as it relates to the Bible. (9) His ethnographic descriptions of life in the societies, communities, and cities of the afterlife in eternity, such as those of heaven and hell, are unique in the annals of literature and science. Swedenborg observed hundreds of times that upon death of the physical body, the remaining spiritual body is "resuscitated" and awakened within 48 hours and continues life in the new spiritual environment, no longer connected to the physical world.

Swedenborg has had a significant influence on the ideas of key Western philosophers, poets, and humanists. The list of documented names include Goethe, Heine, Kant, Schelling, Tennyson, Blake, Coleridge, Dostoevsky, T. Carlyle, Emerson, Henry and William James, Jung, Helen Keller, R. Frost, and many more. (10) At the same time it is noteworthy that Swedenborg's name does not appear in history of science textbooks, as does the name of Descartes who was a contemporary of Swedenborg living in Sweden. (11)

One reason for the absence of Swedenborg in the history of science literature may be that his theistic and dualist system and concepts do not fit anywhere in the 'line of descent' in the history of ideas for the past two centuries in science. Was he scientist or mystic? Was his expertise in engineering, psychology, or theology? Was his ethnographic method allegorical, intuitive or empirical?

At this point however, many features of Swedenborg's theistic psychology and spiritual ethnography are being extended and applied to psychology (12), spirituality (13), physics (14), and biology. (15) These recent developments indicate that the strict materialism of modern science that has largely excluded Swedenborg's work until now may be entering a new phase of reception.

Swedenborg's Substantive Dualism

The nature of consciousness as related to the mind-body issue has not been satisfactorily explained or understood according to a thorough survey of proposals. (16) Nondualist, monistic, or physicalistic explanations of mind cannot disentangle the material from the mental, or the neuron from the feeling, without reducing the mental to the physical by making the two identical, or else deriving the mental from the physical. (17) Such a material neural-based definition of mind and consciousness is inherently incapable of explaining what non-material or mental can be when it is considered in itself rather than as a derivative phenomenon, or as something emergent without its own body structures and anatomy. It has not been sufficiently recognized that mind, when experience is not reduced to the material brain or body, must be understood within a dualist explanatory perspective which offers a modality of discourse that is not material. The purpose of this article is to contribute to the formulation of such dualist discourse concerning mind, consciousness, and spiritual concepts that have traditionally been examined in literature, philosophy and religion but less so in science and psychology.

Substantive dualism is an expression proposed in this article as an appropriate subject heading for Swedenborg's concepts and religious theistic system. The expression references a rational and systematic explanation for what might be the interaction mechanism between immaterial mind and material body. This is the dimension that was lacking in Descartes and possibly why his dualism was irrelevant to the materialist outlook of modern psychology. On the other hand, Swedenborg's dual consciousness allowed him to overcome this theoretical weakness by introducing the concept of the spiritual body, which he described as being identical to the physical body in all respects of anatomy and function, *but not in substance and origin.*

According to this account human beings are born with two functionally interrelated bodies, one physical and the other spiritual, one in the physical world of time, the other in the spiritual world apart from time. Each body is composed of the elements available in the body's environment. The material elements that compose the physical body originate from the sun and stars of the natural world. The immaterial elements that compose the spiritual body originate from the sun of the spiritual world. Hence Swedenborg's dualism may be rightly called "substantive" to reflect the idea that each world contains its own substances that serve as building blocks for the environment and its objects.

A difficult concept to comprehend when thinking within a materialist framework is Swedenborg's idea that the sun of the spiritual world is composed of Divine love and truth defined as mental substance having always existed in God in infinite variety. Spiritual heat streaming from the spiritual sun is defined as *love-substance*, while spiritual light that is adjoined to it is defined as *truth-substance*.

Swedenborg argued that it was unscientific and irrational to think that God created the universe out of nothing, from which it is impossible to derive anything. His solution was to introduce the idea of mental substance that is "uncreate" and has always existed in God. Love-substance and truth-substance streaming out from the spiritual sun into creation provides the building blocks from which the objects and environments of both worlds are made of. Since love-substance and truth-substance refer to mental states and experience, the amazing conclusion follows that *God created the spiritual world of eternity and the natural world of time out of mental substance originating in God.*

The idea of mental substance is novel in Western science and literature. It is more usual to define thoughts and feelings as emergent epiphenomena of the physical brain. (18) But in Swedenborg's substantive dualism the opposite relationship is proposed and described. The anatomical organs of the physical body are defined as derivative material structures whose form and function originate from the spiritual body, which is primary. The two structures, one material the other spiritual, are functionally locked to each other by means of the built-in law of correspondences that is in place as part of creation. The mental functions of the spiritual body are primary and act as cause while the physical organs are merely derivative and react as an effect. There is therefore nothing alive in the physical body as such which is made of inert matter.

When the physical body's material organs deteriorate from injury or sickness, they are then no longer capable of corresponding to the activity of the spiritual body and the dying process is precipitated. Swedenborg observed that this anatomical process of decoupling or separation from the physical body lasts about 48 hours after which the individual awakens in the consciousness of the spiritual body only, and continues life in this new medium or environment.

Swedenborg's theistic and substantive dualism is focused on the details of how God maintains the dual universe to be in correspondence to each other. This is the opposite idea of an independent reality for the natural and spiritual worlds. Swedenborg's framework couples the events in the two worlds strictly one by one, event-by-event, sub-part-by-sub-part. No event or function can exist in the natural world that is not produced by a corresponding event or function in the spiritual world. God creates and manages every object or event in the natural world by means of a corresponding object or event in the spiritual world. The relationship is described as that between cause and effect. Every natural event is an effect and every spiritual event is a cause. This built-in cause-effect relation between discrete layers of creation is called *correspondence*.

God creates all things that exist by sequential levels from highest (or inmost) to lowest (or outmost). Each discrete level is different from the others and the levels or layers are arranged top down, from closest to perfection on top, downward to less and less perfection, until it reaches the outmost or lowest layer where it is inert and devoid of living substance and intelligence. In this substantive system of creation God governs events by managing the series of layers from top to bottom, so that a higher layer causes a corresponding event to occur in the next lower layer. This rationality and predictability in how Divine Providence works allows us to become more aware of God's intention and goal in creation, which holds up human beings as its central feature. God created the dual universe for the sake of human beings and there is nothing created that does not support and promote their needs and happiness. As Swedenborg would put it, everything that exists must ultimately have a human use.

The discrete layers of creation are unified by the Divine Law of Correspondences. Swedenborg states that in most ancient times the oldest science, which was called the Science of Correspondences, was the chief doctrinal study and application of religion. (19) Religion was defined as living one's life in accordance with God's commandments. To do this appropriately it was necessary to identify correctly what God commands. It was acknowledged that God gives revelations of truth in Sacred Scripture and that without adequate interpretation it was not possible to fully understand Sacred Scripture. The science of correspondences of the ancients was transmitted from generation to generation and offered a way of interpreting Sacred Scripture in a spiritual way. This then formed the basis for the rules of life.

By Divine Providence the knowledge of correspondences was forgotten in later ages and Swedenborg asserts that it was his divinely given task to reveal once more the laws of correspondences and to demonstrate that the Old and New Testaments were written in correspondences of meaning, with the spiritual layer lying hidden within the natural or literal. (20) He published two-dozen volumes in Latin on this stupendous exegetical demonstration by meticulously analyzing word-by-word, and verse-by-verse, the text of *Genesis*, *Exodus*, and *Revelations*, in addition to thousands of passages from the rest of the Old and New Testaments that he presents incidentally. (21) These are the "*Secrets of Heaven*" that he was given to reveal after the laws of correspondences had been forgotten from human history and memory. The significance of Swedenborg's analysis of the Old and New Testaments and his method of correspondences will be further discussed in the section on Swedenborg's scientific approach to Bible exegesis that is presented below.

The laws of correspondences are cause-effect interactions between layers of creation that exist in non-continuous or *discrete degrees* relative to each other. There is no possibility of a direct interaction or continuous connection between physical structure and mental structure as these belong to different worlds and are each made of the materials and substances from their respective worlds. They are in discrete degrees of existence and they interact only by built-in correspondence from creation. (22) In relation to each other the world of causes is the mental-spiritual world while the world of effects is the physical or natural world. Hence *the substantive spiritual body causes by correspondence the events occurring in the material physical body*. This explanation excludes the possibility of the physical, which is inert and material, acting on the mental, which is living and spiritual. Effects cannot act upon causes, but only causes upon effects.

In materialist science it is common to discuss natural events as being caused by other natural events. However, according to theistic dualism the relations between all natural events to each other are merely correlations, not true cause-effect interactions. In theistic science every natural object or function has a prior cause that is in the spiritual world, which is also to be called the mental world since both are created out of Divine love-substance and truth-substance, *these being mental objects*. Things prior (like causes) have no *direct* connection with things posterior (like effects), as these two are in discrete layers of substance, not continuous. Objects in discrete degrees or layers correspond to each other by built-in laws of creation of the universe. In the top-down series of created layers the substances in any layer are causative of the events in the immediately lower layer. In this way all the layers of existence are integrated and function synchronously together, starting from the highest layer, which immediately surrounds the spiritual sun by which God created the dual universe, and ending with the lowest layer, which contains the inert objects of the physical world.

Swedenborg's religious psychology is fully theistic and opens up a new scientific discourse involving rational Laws of Divine Providence by which God manages all events in a unified cause-effect series. These series and laws are discoverable by systematic analysis of the spiritual sense of Sacred Scripture. More will be said below on this amazing claim.

All people, animals, and plants possess physical anatomical structures that are uniquely created to be in perfect correspondence with inflowing life from the Divine. Swedenborg points out that it is not rational to suppose that God can give away life to others so that these others now have life of their own. If this were so God would no longer be omnipotent. God cannot give away life to created things but can continuously flow in so hat it appears to the individual that life is his own or her own. Hence the more scientific idea is to define life in terms of Divine love and rationality that stream out as substance from God through the spiritual sun and are received continuously by the mental anatomical structures of the spiritual body of each human being. As long as this living inflow of mental substance persists, the inert objects capable of receiving it appear to be alive and to function as an independent individual. This may be thought to be analogous to a light bulb that seems to have its own power, when yet it receives it continuously from the electric line.

At the same time God insures individuality and uniqueness for every human being in two ways. First, each individual is created as a unique soul and spiritual body, and receives the inflow of Divine love-substance and truth-substance uniquely and differently than any other individual. Second, God through His omnipotence and omnipresence maintains and sustains mental freedom to think and act in accordance with one's loves and affections. These two things together explain how the same Divine influx has different consequences in individuals.

The human anatomical form is the most perfect in creation because it is an image and likeness of God the Divine Human and is thereby created to receive the inflowing Divine truth-substance more genuinely in the powers of rationality and intelligence. And similarly the organ of the will is created to receive the inflowing Divine love-substance that provides the powers of freedom to intend and act according to one's own love. Human consciousness is made of this intelligence and freedom acting together in life. Animals have a lower consciousness that is restricted to sensory input interacting with the built-in instinctive mechanisms. The "instinctive" feature in animals is actually an expression of the built-in laws of correspondences between spiritual laws and physical. The seemingly intelligent behavior of animals and their ability to survive is due to this spiritual influx moment by moment as the animal acts.

Swedenborg's mental anatomy or spiritual physiology was detailed and specific thanks to the expertise he acquired by a careful study of the work of anatomists of his day. (23) Mental activity occurs at different anatomical layers in the spiritual body. Higher layers provide the experience of consciousness through spiritual-rational and celestial-rational concepts and principles of perception and understanding, while lower layers are populated by natural and sensual concepts and explanatory principles that are unavoidably culture-bound, time-bound and material. In this system of thought, consciousness is a spiritual physiological activity of the organic spiritual body. This will be further explored below.

The Dual Universe and the Dual Mind

Swedenborg defined God's mind as Human Divine Love and Wisdom (or truth), in whom infinite distinct things make one. God is the Divine Human, the only Human Itself from eternity to eternity, without beginning nor end, who created finite human beings in God's "own Image and Likeness". Human is defined as the ability to "act from freedom according to reason". (24) This rational ability in the understanding or intellectual faculty is joined to freedom in the will or voluntary faculty, and acting together as one they constitute the essence of being human.

God is the original Human itself. God is the infinite Human who is omnipresent. God is Human as well as Divine because God creates the world and its objects from infinite Divine Love, which is freedom in God's will according to infinite Divine Wisdom, which is rationality in God's understanding. The human body, whose shape or form is familiar to us, is the embodiment of the human mind. (25) The mind or spiritual body is in the perfect human form. The physical body displays the human form because that form or structure is a correspondence (or image) of the human mind. The bodies of animals are not in the human form because their mind is not human given that they do not act from reason but from innate instinct. Their freedom is to act according to this built-in knowledge and its learned extensions and adaptations, and this is not real freedom, which requires rational decision-making in a symbolic cognitive medium. (26)

Swedenborg's theistic cosmology specifies that the first phase of creating the universe was the coming into being of the spiritual sun, which is the first Divine Proceeding (or outgoing) and the source of all further creations. God created the universe by means of the spiritual sun, which contains love-substance in infinite variety and truth-substance in the form of wisdom and rationality. These two uncreate and eternal substances in God are continuously streaming out of the spiritual sun and thereby create and sustain the atmospheres and spaces of the two worlds. Swedenborg points to the correspondence between the physical sun or stars, being the origin of planet earth and all its matters and atmospheres, and the spiritual sun, being the origin of the spiritual world and all its mental objects and contents.

But while the physical heat and light of the natural sun are inert, lifeless, and purely material existing in space and time, the spiritual heat and light of the spiritual sun are purely substantial existing apart from physical space and time. That which is created with material substance in physical space and time is called natural, material, and temporal, while that which is created with spiritual substance apart from time and physical space, is called spiritual, substantial, and eternal.

The goal of theistic science is to account for all events and phenomena in both worlds by reconstructing the cause-effect sequence of steps by which God creates and manages events through intermediate layers of relative functioning and integration. (27) What is of fundamental interest here is the notion that God sequentially initiates each successive layer of creation starting from the spiritual sun, and when that creation is sequentially completed all the layers now function and exist simultaneously. (28) Analytically therefore we can reverse this process as if we could see the layers of existence of any natural object. Considering a piece of rock for instance, we can assert that its inmost layer of existence is substantive, not material. God creates the visible material plane as an externalized layer that functions to cover, protect, and exhibit the substantive layer that is discretely within the rock, apart from physical space and time.

The spiritual substance of the inmost layer closest to the spiritual sun is spiritual heat adjoined to spiritual light. (29) And from this comes the following amazing revelation:

Spiritual heat is Divine love-substance or "good" (used as a noun as in 'goodness'), while spiritual light is Divine wisdom or truth-substance. In other words, the inmost layer of the rock, and the rest of the physical universe, is Divine Love and Truth. (30) What is material substance is constructed and generated by God out of what is mental substance (i.e., love and truth). The more layers are externalized and distanced from the spiritual sun the more they become composite and gross, until at the ultimates they are inert matter and incapable of receiving any life.

In theistic dualism God is present in all places "apart from physical space, and in all times apart from time". (31) From the rational perspective in order to create physical space God had to be apart from that space, and in order to create time God had to be apart from time. It follows that God's omnipresence in the physical world is possible apart from space but is not possible in space, and similarly with time. (32) God creates the universe by means of the infinite living substance of good (or love) adjoined to truth (or wisdom and rationality) that in God are unified as one. (33) As this Divine spiritual substance proceeds from God and is exteriorized into creation

61

through the spiritual sun, it puts on composite layers from each of the layers through which God creates things from top (or inmost) to downward (or outmost).

A physical object remains in its created function or purpose as long as its external composite material shell remains intact so that it corresponds to the internal spiritual form. Life is the living Divine love-substance adjoined to truth-substance that we receive through the anatomical structures of the soul and its spiritual body. Our physical body in time and space corresponds in form and activity to our spiritual body that is in the spiritual world and thus apart from time and physical space. But when the physical body is no longer capable due to injury or malfunction to correspond in receptive form to the spiritual body, the dying process is initiated. By this activity God anatomically disentangles the spiritual body from the physical body, whereupon life and consciousness of the individual continue to eternity in the spiritual world of the afterlife. (34)

This makes clear that the substantive atmosphere of the spiritual-mental world is living and is in the organic human form. Thus it is that the spiritual world of the afterlife is the same as the mental world of humanity. There is only one mental world for human beings just as there is only one physical space for the natural world, be it between galaxies or within the atom. Every individual is born into that one universal mental world through the spiritual body. The spiritual world of eternity that is made of Divine love and truth is therefore the same as the mental world with which everyone is already very familiar, as will be further discussed below. We are born into eternity and our mental life is there now.

Swedenborg defines the substance of spiritual heat as uncreate living substance of love that exists infinitely in the will of the Divine Human. (35) This aspect of Swedenborg's religious system is unique in philosophical literature and history and may be called anatomical organic substantive theistic dualism, or simply theistic dualism for short. (36) The spiritual world of the afterlife is thus the world of eternity apart from time-space and is constructed of God's living and uncreate substances proceeding from Him through the spiritual sun. The infinite and invisible God the Divine Human becomes visible in a more exteriorized form or appearing (epiphany). Swedenborg insisted that the idea of a universe created "out of nothing" is a logical absurdity because out of nothing, nothing can be constructed or derived. (37)

All objects that exist and have a quality or function must have structure and form, or else they are nothing. God's infinite and uncreate spiritual substance of love (spiritual heat) and truth (spiritual light) constitute the building elements of all that exists in reality in both worlds. Divine Human love is the inmost substance in the infrastructure of every existing object, while truth-substance is its intermediate or outward layer, just as physical light is the outer form of physical heat, the two acting together as one. (38)

Since love and wisdom are both human and mental, the surprising conclusion is that the created universe is constructed on an infrastructure of living Divine spiritual and mental substance in eternity (apart from time and space). To say it another way, temporary physical time-space and matter are constructed out of permanent mental-spiritual substance that is apart from time-space. The time/space/matter continuum is an inert outward shell capable of receiving and holding within itself the inner continuum of eternity/love/truth. The mental/spiritual/human world from within is therefore the basis out of which the physical world is constructed from without through God's built-in laws of correspondence between discrete layers. (39)

This is a unique and striking aspect of Swedenborg's religious-anatomical system, namely that *the spiritual world of the afterlife of eternity is one and the same as the mental world that is so familiar to every human being from birth.* This is because the building blocks of reality are from the living substance of Divine Human love and wisdom, and these are mental or spiritual objects that have a mental or spiritual existence in eternity apart from matter, time, and space. The inmost structure of any physical object is actually the living mental substance of Divine love and wisdom. The particular objects of the mind – such as sensations, perceptions, thoughts, emotions, feelings, intentions –are not in physical space, not in physical time, not in physical matter. Feeling, thinking, and sensing are activities in the spiritual world where the mind functions as a spiritual body with which we are born and which develops and matures with experience and learning. (40)

Swedenborg's scientific-theistic system is complete and absolute, defining reality as created by a perfectly rational and omnipotent Human God who is the only power, the only intelligence, and is the First Cause of all that exists in reality. God created the dual universe not "out of nothing", but by exteriorizing His own infinite Divine inner substance into finite creation. He did this through the intermediary of the spiritual sun, which is God's own living substance proceeding into creation. (41)

The dual universe was created by means of the action of the spiritual sun whose heat and light create discrete layers of substantive atmospheres or discrete layers in which created objects can exist, each at their own level or degree of living and activity. The whole layered system is unified as one, acting as one unit from top to bottom. This unification by immediate Divine influx is therefore a continuous creation. (42) The universe would instantly fail and vanish were the Divine influx to stop, just as a light bulb fails when the electricity is switched off.

Every person's mind is formed at birth out of a complete set of the anatomical layers or degrees of the spiritual-mental world. The individual's mind is an "image and likeness" of God's mind and in consequence of this correspondence human consciousness can be elevated and lowered, and elevated again, throughout these discrete anatomical layers.

The individual's mind matures through the acquisition and incorporation of ideas and intentions that are formed out of each anatomical layer. Concepts formed in the lower natural "sensuous" layer of the mind are closely associated with the physical body and its fixed structure in time and space. Concepts formed in the higher rational layers are spiritual and universal, thus abstracted from physical time-space. (43) At each mental anatomical layer, consciousness operates in accordance with its concept formation and consequent level of perception, awareness, and understanding.

As the anatomical layers of spiritual atmospheres progress further down into the exteriorizing sequence of creation and away in perfection from the spiritual sun, they become more compounded of earlier layers and consequently less reactive to spiritual substance acting on them, until at last the substantive layers become fully "materialized" and inert in comparison to the earlier living activity. They become inert solid physical matter. These solidified or materialized layers are constructed and fixed in space and time. (44) It is the physical-natural world. The determination of their purposeful evolution and their goal-oriented progressive changes over time, are not anywhere in themselves but are induced in them by being maintained in continuous correspondence to the mental-spiritual events that are their causes.

All creation or reality is defined as a unified system in which the layers of atmospheres and their contents operate on one another downward (or outward) as cause and effect. Since a cause without an effect is nothing, and an effect without a cause is impossible, therefore all layers of the dual universe are integrated, coordinated, and operate simultaneously as one system or unit. Any real thing that exists or occurs must exist from a cause, and this cause from a still prior cause, until the First Cause, which is God who always exited and has no beginning. Since God is infinite and cannot be divided, it follows that the Divine Human quality or presence is the same in all the layers. God is present in every layer fully and equally. (45)

It is the structure of the anatomical layer and its unique variable mental objects that determine how the Divine Human spiritual substance is received and retained. (46) For example, the sun of the natural world shines equally on the different plants in an area, and yet its heat and light penetrate differently into each depending on its cell structure and function. God through spiritual heat or love from the spiritual sun, together with spiritual light or wisdom, enters equally in all souls and human minds, yet each person uniquely receives this Divine inflow, filtering and contextualizing it moment by moment, with the freedom to modify it, reject it, or turn it into its exact opposite.

The system of corresponding layers makes it rationally clear how God's omnipresence is possible, since what is from God cannot be divided or separated from God. It remains fully God within each discrete layer and object, though not part of it but apart from it. Therefore, by means of the spiritual substance of Divine love adjoined to Divine truth, God is present everywhere and in each individual object equally, largest and smallest. The highest anatomical layer in the individual's mind (called "celestial-rational" consciousness) is closest in the inflow from the spiritual sun and consequently the greatest in perfection. This means that it is more authentic and less covered up by general features, and is therefore more perfect in its representation of the genuine love and wisdom in the Divine Human. Below this celestial-rational layer lies the spiritual-rational layer with its proper consciousness, and in the third or lowest region is the "sensual-natural" layer in which thoughts and concerns are closest to the physical body and world. (47)

One might consider why human beings need to be born with a temporary physical body in the natural world since the mind is fully in the spiritual body from birth. Swedenborg explains that the spiritual body needs a natural containant or external border in order for its inner anatomical layers to remain fixed and permanent. (48) The two-day dying and resuscitation process separates the physical body but retains a thin natural covering composed of "the finest substances" of the physical world. This covering is called the limbus (= skin or "border" in Latin). After resuscitation from the dying process our spiritual body or mind is permanently fixed through the material quality of the limbus. (49) This explains why character change or regeneration cannot take place after death given that the baseline anatomical structures and fibers are fixed in the limbus. Everything we loved while being attached to the physical body remains in our spiritual body fixed to eternity.

According to this explanation repentance and a change of heart when the person is seriously ill and nearing death is of no effect for salvation because after resuscitation the person is still attached to the loves and habits of a lifetime. Being then in total freedom, the free choice is to enter more deeply into the loves that are anatomically imprinted on the mind's body. Regeneration that is effective must involve a mental struggle against one's habits of selfish or anti-social loves. The purpose of temptations is to allow the individual an opportunity to reject as-if from self a former love and consequently to struggle not to give in or to fulfill that love in in intention and action. In this as-of self struggle it is God (not the person) who supplies the spiritual power to resist an anatomically ingrained love. Once again this principle shows to what amazing extent God is intimately involved in an individual's life and growth from birth to eternity.

Swedenborg reviews the belief by many that at death the "soul" goes into a waiting mode until the "resurrection" event when the physical world will be instantaneously dissolved and renewed, and new physical bodies will be supplied to the waiting souls who will then continue life in the natural world in an earthly paradise. He points out that this belief is based on a literal reading of some passages in the Old Testament where the day of judgment and the resurrection of all is so described. But in the spiritual sense of these passages it is clear that the resurrection of the physical body is not meant but the resuscitation of the spirit in the spiritual world. Swedenborg brings forth numerous other passages in the Old and New Testaments where this meaning is made clear even in the literal sense. Swedenborg adds that accepting this description is not harming regenerating people who take these verses to be literally true. After resuscitation they are informed of the spiritual meaning in these verses and they are able without difficulty to expand their view accordingly since they have not formed for themselves life practices that are contrary to good.

But this is not so with those who have not been regenerating and have continued to progress in their inherited selfish and anti-social character loves. Being in total social and mental freedom after resuscitation the individuals who are imbued with these negative loves reject any information and truths that are contrary to those loves. Hence they are unwilling to undergo the struggles of regeneration even in the afterlife. Swedenborg's central religious theme is that the truths acquired from the Word and the faith based on it, is not sufficient for salvation because there is no love for them to permanently fix them in our mental anatomy. These truths will be rejected after resuscitation because they do not accord with the selfish and anti-community loves that have become their habit of thinking, intending, and doing. Swedenborg confirms this by direct observation having entered into discussions with "the recently departed" about what they believe and what they are now seeking. Swedenborg writes:

> That which anyone does from love remains inscribed on his heart, for love is the fire of life, thus is the life of everyone. Consequently such as is the love, such is the life; and such as is the life, thus such as is the love, such is the whole man as to soul and as to body. (Swedenborg, AC 10740)

Hanegraaff refers to Swedenborg's works as "*a huge reservoir of religious ideas and concepts, from which emerged a comprehensive worldview of startling originality and internal consistency*". (54) In his review and discussion of Kant's relationship to Swedenborg's religious concepts Hanegraaff points out that Kant and Swedenborg agree that human beings cannot 'discover' the truth about God and the afterlife since there is no direct connection between the two worlds and no possibility of direct observation. Kant concludes that therefore we cannot attain any direct knowledge of heaven. Perhaps Kant was not sufficiently familiar with Swedenborg's many volumes to realize that Swedenborg presents the "secrets of heaven" not as something his natural mind discovered but as something that was granted him by God through the preparation and opening of his spiritual mind that he might have dual consciousness simultaneously in both worlds.

The present article discussed Swedenborg's concepts of the dual universe and the rational laws by which God manages or sustains the universe. These concepts and notions are direct extractions from the spiritual sense of the Word. In this sense Swedenborg's work is discretely different from other philosophers, theologians, and scientists who are presenting their ideas and principles discovered from reflection, study, and observation of the natural world and of the Bible in its literal sense. Swedenborg was mindful by Divine commandment that he should not include in the *Secrets of Heaven* anything whatsoever that originated in others, in the natural world, or in his own thinking about others and the world. *Swedenborg therefore was not a true philosopher like the others of his time who wrote about their own ideas in philosophy, science and religion.*

Some biographers have called Swedenborg a "revelator" and others "a mystic". But this term implies something mysterious and unscientific. Perhaps better fitting terms for Swedenborg would include theistic scientist, ethnographer of the afterlife, or the man with dual consciousness. As for Swedenborg he called himself "*Servant of the Lord Jesus Christ*" which is part of the extended Latin title of *Secrets of Heaven*.

In this article Swedenborg's claims about what he saw and witnessed through dual consciousness *is taken at face value* as one would a knowledgeable traveller's ethnographic report of a far off island or planet. Doing this sidesteps the long-standing literary controversy about whether Swedenborg was allegorical in his descriptions of heaven and hell (like Blake), or delusional in his thinking as a scientist (almost no one called him a fraud). Some of the influential philosophers of his time and afterwards who saw some but not all of Swedenborg's publications, like Oetinger, Kant, Emerson, and others (55), ultimately concluded in their official statements that Swedenborg was delusional and almost nothing that he wrote can be trusted to agree with enlightened reason.

Nevertheless, Swedenborg's proposal that the *Old Testament* must have a spiritual meaning as well as a natural meaning solves a difficult problem with which many devout readers have had to contend with in their study of the *Old* and *New Testaments*.

Swedenborg collected hundreds of passages in the *Old Testament* in which the literal sense says that God is angry and plans to punish and even to enjoy it on account of people's willful wickedness to each other. In contrast in other places it is stated that God is pure Mercy and never gets angry or plans evil. Furthermore, numerous passages in Moses and the Prophets appear as an incomprehensible pile up of words on top of each other, as for example in Jeremiah (48):

> I know its anger, says Jehovah, and it is not steadfast, and its falsities do not make for right. Therefore I will howl over Moab and will cry out to the whole of Moab. From the weeping of Jazer I will weep for you, O vine of Sibmah. Your branches passed over the sea, they reached as far as the sea of Jazer; on your summer fruits and on your vintage the vastator has fallen. Therefore My heart is moved over Moab like pipes. Woe to you, O Moab!

Or in Ezekiel 39:17-21:

> Thus saith the Lord Jehovih; Thou son of man, Speak unto the fowl of every wing, and to every beast of the field. Assemble yourselves and come; gather yourselves on every side to my sacrifice that I do sacrifice for you, even a great sacrifice upon the mountains of Israel, that ye may eat flesh, and drink blood. Ye shall eat the flesh of the mighty, and drink the blood of the princes of the earth... Ye shall eat fat till ye be full, and drink blood till ye be drunken, of my sacrifice which I sacrifice for you. Thus ye shall be filled at my table with horse and chariot, with the mighty man and with every man of war ... Thus I will set my glory among the nations.

Given many such puzzling and disturbing passages throughout the Word it is important to examine whether Swedenborg's proposal of a double sense in the Old Testament can rationally resolve the incoherence of the literal sense. Swedenborg painstakingly shows that a spiritual context or meaning can *always* be added to the literal sense of any verse or expression in the Bible. When the reader adds the spiritual context to the expression or verse the combined meaning is enhanced and deepened allowing a rational and universal perspective on what appears in the literal sense as merely an assertion about some historical individual or some minor event occurring in some geographical location.

Some who have criticized and rejected Swedenborg's method of exegesis, as for instance Oetinger and Kant, and later, Emerson (56), have not apparently taken the opportunity to examine the full details of how the spiritual sense enriches and restores the holiness of the literal Word. Swedenborg takes 20 volumes in Latin to make the case giving the analysis of just three books of the Christian Bible: *Genesis*, *Exodus*, and *Revelations*. Perhaps it's too much to expect of most critics to make a careful study of such length and intensity and so they reacted and judged based on a partial awareness of the data.

I have examined and studied the 20 volumes in detail. There is no room here to discuss the assessment except to state my conclusion that Swedenborg's demonstration of a spiritual layer of meaning within the literal of the *Old* and *New Testaments* is completely transparent, rational, and accurate. (57) It is especially remarkable that there is a deep enrichment of consciousness of God and of God's participation in the world when the literal sense is given a spiritual context. The result is a strengthening of one's sense of the holiness of the Word, thus the opposite of what some, like Oetinger had feared, who supposed that the derived spiritual meaning makes void the integrity and holiness of the literal. As Hanegraaff has suggested this appears to be a misunderstanding by Oetinger perhaps due to insufficient familiarity with Swedenborg's writings. Indeed, Swedenborg has stated numerous times that the literal sense remains holy and is not weakened by a recognition of the spiritual sense within it, and also that all the historical details it mentions are true facts. (58)

> In these chapters which contain true historical narratives every single word and statement means in the internal sense something altogether different from what is meant in the sense of the letter. Nevertheless the historical details themselves are representative. 'Abram', who is dealt with first, in general represents the Lord, and specifically the celestial man. 'Isaac', who is dealt with after that, likewise in general represents the Lord, and specifically the spiritual man; and Jacob' too in general represents the Lord, and specifically the natural man. Thus they represent things which are the Lord's, things which belong to His kingdom, and those which belong to the Church.
>
> As stated already, the narratives contained here draw on true history; that is to say, Jehovah did in fact speak to Abram as described; the land of Canaan was promised to him as an inheritance; he was in fact commanded as described to arrange a heifer, she-goat, ram, turtle dove and fledgling; birds of prey came down on the carcasses; a deep sleep came over him, and in that sleep a horror of darkness; and when the sun

had set he did in fact see what looked like a smoking furnace with a flaming torch passing between the parts; besides all the other details mentioned. These events are historically true, but even so every single one, down to the smallest event that took place, is representative; and the actual words used to describe those events, down to the smallest part of a letter, carry a spiritual meaning, that is, every single detail has an internal sense within it. For every single detail in the Word is inspired, and being inspired cannot derive from other than a heavenly origin; that is, celestial and spiritual things lie concealed in its inner recesses. If this were not so it could not possibly be the Word of the Lord.

Sacred Scripture and Theistic Psychology

Swedenborg was a man with a unique mission. His God-given task was to make Bible readers, scholars, and worshippers aware that there is a spiritual sense in the Old and New Testaments. This sense lies hidden within the literal and historical meaning of each verse, expression, name, or number. He was an impeccable scientist deeply committed to rationality and experimentation, and to the empirical method of observation. He strove to achieve consistency in unified theories from several branches of science. He therefore proceeded with the notion that the method of spiritual-natural correspondences employed in his cosmology of the world must also be applicable to the text of the Bible inasmuch as God was the architect of both. This he accomplished by painstakingly showing that the text in the Old and New Testaments was written by Divine Providence in layers of meaning representing the layers of consciousness in the human mind, namely, natural, rational, and spiritual.

Although fully successful, the demonstration and elucidation of the spiritual meanings in *Sacred Scripture* was not sufficient from a scientific perspective. There had to be a way of empirically confirming the spiritual content of the text. This opportunity was given him by Divine Providence when at the height of his scientific career he suddenly found himself overnight with dual consciousness. And this perception lasted for 27 years until his death. He was now able to see directly around him in the spiritual environment what each expression in the sacred text contained hidden as its spiritual sense.

Swedenborg's work is to prove that the spiritual sense in *Sacred Scripture* coalesces into a rational account of creation and God's relationship to human beings. Given that Swedenborg's work is universal it may justly be called the foundation of theistic psychology. When we think about God and the world at the level of our natural mind we are synchronizing with our reading of the literal and historical-cultural sense of God's Word. But when we raise our consciousness to the rational mind we are able to think about the world and about our relationship to God in more universal terms through the rationale of spiritual correspondences. This allows us to restore "the Bible that was lost" (52) since the historical-cultural accounts in themselves, without the spiritual context, have less power and relevance as the centuries proceed from the original events.

A final question will now be raised. Is the work of Swedenborg about religion or about theistic psychology? The answer is "both". This may be seen by considering the interaction effects between the spiritual sense and the literal sense of *Sacred Scripture*.

The perspective presented in this book is that the spiritual sense of universal *Sacred Scripture* throughout the various religions and cultures constitutes the body of knowledge of theistic psychology. (59) In contrast, the totality of the literal sense constitutes religion. Wherever there is a religion there is a specific *Sacred Scripture*. Religion would not be feasible without some *Sacred Scripture*. By Divine Providence there is provided a variety of religions suitable or adapted to the mental needs of all cultures and individuals. All genuine religions are serviceable for salvation and have been provided their own *Sacred Scripture* in a language, style, and cultural theme that is acceptable to believers.

Since all genuine *Sacred Scripture* is given by God the method of correspondences necessarily applies to their text. I made a preliminary test of this expectation by analyzing the correspondential sense of a few selections from Yoga, the Mudras, the Bhagavad Gita, and the Upanishads. (60) My preliminary conclusion was that the spiritual sense hidden within the literal of these various religious texts overlaps significantly in topic and content with theistic science that is based on the spiritual sense of the *Old* and *New Testaments*. Of course this hypothesis needs to be further researched in a more systematic way in order to confirm or disconfirm it.

The topic, content, and message in the spiritual sense of the Word are precisely what Swedenborg perceived through his spiritual consciousness about the spiritual world. When this sense is collated and unified there emerges a rational account of creation and human beings that may be called theistic science. By learning and reflecting on the content of theistic science anyone can now perceive and understand the knowledge that Swedenborg acquired through his dual consciousness.

We may list several ways in which the spiritual sense of *Sacred Scripture* interacts and affects the literal sense, or to put it in other words, the ways in which theistic science can affect religion.

Function *1.*
The spiritual sense helps to resolve contradictions in the literal sense.

For instance, when the text says that God is angry, punishes, and casts into hell (Psalm 7:11; 1 Kings 11:9–10; 17:18; John 2:13–16; Mark 3:4–5; Isaiah 10:22, 23), versus when it says that God never gets angry and is merciful to all. In the spiritual sense one puts together two ideas about God. Once is that He is pure Mercy and Love from His inmost Being, and therefore can never feel anger. The other is that the literal meaning refers to how God appears to the mind of those who reject His Commandments. The anger is in the appearance to them, not in God. Supplying the spiritual context for the meaning of God being angry acts to restore and clarify the spiritual message, as is done by Swedenborg when explicating the spiritual sense of "long-suffering with angers" in Exodus 34:6:

> *"Long-suffering with angers." That this signifies the Divine clemency, is evident from the signification of "long-suffering with angers," when said of Jehovah, as being that He long endures the evils of man, for to be "long-suffering" denotes to endure and bear for a long time; and "angers" denote the evils with man. The reason why "angers," when said of Jehovah, denote the evils with man, is that evil becomes angry, and good never; and evil is with man and never with the Lord, for the Lord is good itself. Nevertheless anger is attributed to the Lord, because it so appears to a man when he does not obtain what he desires, and when he is punished on account of evil.*

Function 2.
The spiritual sense helps to distinguish genuine doctrine from spurious and false teachings that mislead people.

For instance, there are those who teach that repentance at the last hour of death is sufficient for salvation and admittance into heaven. People who accept this persuasion may plan to postpone a change of heart and life until the last moment. But the spiritual sense clarifies that such repentance is useless for salvation because the person's unregenerated loves remain in the character as selfishness and hatred of others who don't favor them. These evil loves are incompatible with life in heaven where evil loves are not admitted.

Another example is the teaching in some Christian denominations that all go to hell who are not of their religion or who nave not been baptized in the Name of Jesus. But the spiritual sense gives the understanding that entrance into heaven involves one's loves, and if these are the love of God and neighbor, admittance is secured regardless of one's past religion, but if these are loves of self and hatred of the neighbor, being in heaven is impossible. Swedenborg confirmed this with the observation that those who lived by loving others as much as self, and did this from their religion, are willingly instructed about the Lord and the Word regardless of their former beliefs.

Swedenborg compares the Word to the human spirit or form. Most of the literal "body" of the Word is covered over with "clothes" that are appearances of truth such as historical events and prophesies. But a few parts of the Word are like the face and hands and present "naked truths", which means spiritual truths. In other words, the spiritual sense of the Word can sometimes be seen directly in the literal sense: (61)

> The truths of the sense of the letter of the Word are in part not naked truths, but appearances of truth, and are as it were likenesses and comparisons taken from things such as exist in nature, and thus accommodated and adapted to the apprehension of the simple and of little children. But being correspondences they are receptacles and abodes of genuine truth; and are like enclosing and containing vessels, as a crystal cup encloses noble wine, and as a silver plate holds palatable food. ... The naked truths themselves

which are enclosed, held, clothed, and contained, are in the spiritual sense of the Word; and the naked goods are in its celestial sense.

But let this be illustrated from the Word. Jesus said:

> Woe unto you, Scribes and Pharisees, because ye cleanse the outside of the cup and of the platter, but within they are full of extortion and excess. Thou blind Pharisee, cleanse first the inside of the cup and of the platter, that the outside thereof may be clean also (Matt. 23:25-26).

... To "cleanse the inside of the cup and platter" means to purify by means of the Word the interior things which belong to will and thought and thus to love and faith. "That the outside may be clean also" means that in this way, exterior things, which are the actions and the conversation, will have been made pure, for these derive their essence from the interior things.

The disciples of Jesus asked Him "Why do you speak to the people in parables?" Jesus then reveals to them the spiritual sense of the parable of the sower that He had told to a large crowd without any explanations. He refers to the spiritual sense as "the knowledge of the secrets of the kingdom of heaven". (62)

> "Listen then to what the parable of the sower means: When anyone hears the message about the kingdom and does not understand it, the evil one comes and snatches away what was sown in their heart. This is the seed sown along the path.
>
> The seed falling on rocky ground refers to someone who hears the word and at once receives it with joy. But since they have no root, they last only a short time. When trouble or persecution comes because of the word, they quickly fall away. The seed falling among the thorns refers to someone who hears the word, but the worries of this life and the deceitfulness of wealth choke the word, making it unfruitful. But the seed falling on good soil refers to someone who hears the word and understands it. This is the one who produces a crop, yielding a hundred, sixty or thirty times what was sown."

These are naked truths in the Word. From these identifications one can explore like Swedenborg did other passages in the Word that mention sower, seed, path, ground, thorns, soil, crop. Since the spiritual sense of these seven words is directly given one can apply this information to the other passages where these words are used. For instance, "rocky ground" in the spiritual sense corresponds to "trouble or persecution". "Thorns" signify "worries of life". The expression "thorns" appears in the Old Testament, as in the following passage whose spiritual sense Swedenborg explicates: (63)

> When a fire shall go forth, and shall catch hold of thorns, and
> a stack is consumed, or the standing crop, or a field; he that
> kindleth the fire, repaying shall repay. [Exodus 22:5]

> ... "when a fire shall go forth," signifies anger from the affection of evil; "and shall catch hold of thorns," signifies which betakes itself into falsities; "and a stack is consumed," signifies injury to the goods and truths of faith that have been received; "or the standing crop, or a field," signifies also to the goods and truths of faith in their conception; "he that kindleth the fire repaying shall repay," signifies the restoration of what was taken away through anger from the affection of evil.

Here the spiritual meaning of thorns is expanded from "worries of life" to "falsities". Further study of the spiritual sense shows that falsifications or misinterpretations of the Word that are applied to one's life disrupt and oppose character reformation from love of self and one's own to love of neighbor and community. From this one can see that the spiritual sense employed by Jesus in the New Testament is the same as the spiritual sense employed in the Old Testament everywhere. This identity shows the unity that exists between the Old and New Testaments, a unity that cannot be seen when considering the literal meaning only. The analysis of this passage in Exodus also shows a topic that God frequently discusses in the spiritual sense of His Word, namely, the psychology of religion:

- the connection between anger and evil, and how they serve each other
- when applying truths from the Word to one's life there is inner resistance put up by the natural or unregenerate mind
- the mind's tendency to misinterpret what the Word says when the truth is inconvenient
- how the undisciplined love of wealth or power neutralizes the benefits

and protections that religion can give against the permanent adoption of an evil character.

Swedenborg also points to what Jesus said to His disciples after His resurrection teaching them that the Old Testament has a spiritual sense that is about Him:

> The Lord Himself also, after the Resurrection, taught the disciples what had been written concerning Himself in Moses and the Prophets, Luke 24:27, thus that nothing has been written in the Word which does not have regard to Him, to His kingdom, and to the Church. These are the spiritual and celestial things of the Word, but the sense of the letter consists for the most part of worldly, bodily, and earthly images which cannot possibly constitute the Word of the Lord. (64)

Function 3.
The spiritual sense helps to unify all religions by showing their common source.

The literal sense of *Sacred Scripture* in every religion is culture-bound and time-bound. It would not otherwise be accepted. The spiritual sense by itself cannot form a religion precisely because it is culture free, universal, and scientific, as in the case of theistic science. The literal sense of culture-bound texts are historically ingrown and cannot easily be transferred into another culture or location. Adaptation is necessary for acceptance. Consequently religions are often hostile to one another in thought and practice. But this aversion and enmity is cultural, not spiritual. The spiritual sense of Sacred Scripture in all genuine religions overlaps and is compatible with all the others.

Function 4.
The spiritual sense helps to raise consciousness from natural-sensuous to spiritual-rational.

The literal sense of *Sacred Scripture* in all religions is at times used by some people to justify anti-social actions that are destructive of self and community. As against this distortion, the spiritual sense brings greater clarity of perception and reasoning to see when *Sacred Scripture* is misused. The natural sense in itself offers little protection for false doctrines in all religions. Remaining solely in the literal sense of *Sacred Scripture* encourages the logic of natural-sensuous consciousness, which promotes divisions and enmities between and within religious groups. Adding the spiritual sense as a context raises the reasoning level to spiritual-rational consciousness since the ideas in the Word are then applied universally, consistently, and free of the prejudices that culture contains.

Helen Keller was aware of the spiritual sense in the Bible by studying Swedenborg's books published in Braille. (65) Silverman writes in his Introduction to Helen Keller's book "*How I Would Help the World*":

> *Helen believed that bringing Swedenborg's teachings to a world that is "spiritually deaf and blind" would be her greatest service. It would be her attempt to help people discover, as she had, the unlimited treasures she believed were stored up in the Word of God. In doing so, she would help to restore confidence in scripture as a divinely given revelation of God's will. And she would help resist the "evils of unbelief" that shake their confidence in god's unfailing love and guidance.*"

As a result she was moved to write this in her little book titled My Religion "One thing I know that whereas I was blind, now I see." (66)

Reference Notes to Chapter 1

(1) Rose, J., Shotwell, S., & Bertucci, M.L. (2005). *Emanuel Swedenborg: Essays for the New Century Edition on His Life, Work, and Impact*. New York: Swedenborg Foundation.

(2) Hanegraaff, W. J. (2007). *Swedenborg, Oetinger, Kant: Three Perspectives on the Secrets of Heaven (Swedenborg Studies)*. Westchester, PA: Swedenborg Foundation Publishers. (p. 73)

(3) Sigstedt, C. (1952). *The Swedenborg Epic. The Life and Works of Emanuel Swedenborg*. New York: Bookman Associates.

Tafel, R. L. (1890). *Documents Concerning the Life and Character of Emanuel Swedenborg*. London: Swedenborg Society. Copy available online at http://swedenborgdigitallibrary.org/tafel/tafeltc.html Accessed on the Web in May 2014.

Trobridge, G. M. (1976). *Swedenborg: Life and Teaching*. New York: Swedenborg Foundation.

(4) Söderberg, H. (1988). Swedenborg's 1714 airplane. A machine to fly in the air. New York: Swedenborg Foundation.

(5) Gross, C. G. (2009). Three before their time: neuroscientists whose ideas were ignored by their contemporaries. *Experimental Brain Research* 192:321.

Gross, C. G. (2003). Twitches versus movements. A story of motor cortex. *The Neuroscientist* 16: 332-342.

Gross C. G. (1997). Emanuel Swedenborg: A neuroscientist before his time. *The Neuroscientist* 3: 2.

Tubbs, R. S, Riech S., Verma, K., Loukas, M., Mortazavi, M., & Cohen-Gadol, A. (2011). Emanuel Swedenborg (1688-1772): pioneer of neuroanatomy. *Childs Nervous System* Aug;27(8):1353-5.

Fodstad, H. (2001). The neuron theory". *Stereotactic and Functional Neurosurgery*. 77:20-4.

(6) Williams-Hogan, J.K. (2012). The philosophical context of Swedenborg the philosopher—reason and faith, faith and reason—A human project. *The New Philosophy*, July-December Vol. CXV, Nos. 3&4, 325-369.

Thompson, I. (2011). *Starting Science from God: Rational Scientific Theories from Theism*. Pleasanton: Eagle Pearl Press.

James, L. (2008a). *Introduction to Theistic Psychology. Tome III. Correspondences*. Web publication accessed in May 2014.

http://www.soc.hawaii.edu/leonj/theistic/correspondences.htm

James, L. (2008b). *The Organic Mind: Discovering the Mental World of Eternity*. Web publication accessed in May 2014. http://www.soc.hawaii.edu/leonj/mental-psychology-p1.htm

(7) Kant, I. (1766). *Dreams of a Spirit-Seer*. Träume eines Geistersehers, Erläutert durch Träume der Metaphysik. Königsberg: Johann Jacob Kanter. Original German reprinted at: http://www.gutenberg.org/files/36076/36076-h/36076-h.htm Web publication accessed in May 2014.

(8) Brock, E.J. (General Editor). (1988). *Swedenborg and His Influence*. Bryn Athyn, PA: The Academy of the New Church.

Larsen, R. (Editor). (1988). *Emanuel Swedenborg: A Continuing Vision*. New York: Swedenborg Foundation.

(9) Swedenborg's Works mentioned in this article and their standard abbreviations are the following:

> AC: Arcana Coelestia (Secrets of Heaven) (1747-1756)
> AR: Apocalypse Revealed (1766)
> CL: Conjugial Love (1768)
> DLW: Divine Love and Wisdom (1763)
> DP: Divine Providence (1764)
> HH: Heaven and Hell (1758)
> ISB: Interrelationship Between Soul and Body (1769)
> SE: Spiritual Experiences (1747-1763)
> SS: Sacred Scripture (1763)
> TCR: True Christian Religion (1771)

All of Swedenborg's writings can be accessed online at: http://www.sacred-texts.com/swd/index.htm and can be searched at: http://www.heavenlydoctrines.org/dtSearch.html

(10) Brock, E.J. (Ed.). (1989). *Swedenborg and His Influence*. Bryn Athyn, PA: Academy of the New Church Book.

Thompson, I. (2014). Writers Influenced by Swedenborg. Web publication accessed May 2014 http://www.swedenborgstudy.com/articles/history-of-art/writers-influenced.htm

James, W. (1898). Human immortality. Web document reprint copy accessed in May 2014. http://www.soc.hawaii.edu/leonj/theistic/William-James-immortality.htm

(11) Williams-Hogan, J.K. (2012). The philosophical context of Swedenborg the philosopher—reason and faith, faith and reason—A human project. *The New Philosophy*, July-December Vol. CXV, Nos. 3&4, 325-369.

(12) James, L. (2004). *Principles of Theistic Psychology: The Scientific Knowledge of God Extracted from the Correspondential Sense of Sacred Scripture*. Web publication accessed in May 2014. http://e-swedenborg.com/tp/books/theistic/index.htm

James, L. (1998). Overcoming objections to Swedenborg's Writings through the development of scientific dualism. *New Philosophy*, v.CIV n.3 & 4 pp. 153-217. Copy available here: http://swedenborg-philosophy.org/journal/article.php?page=1027&issue=104b Web publication accessed in May 2014.

James, L. (1995). Swedenborg Encyclopedia of Theistic Psychology. The Ideas of Emanuel Swedenborg (1668-1772) Expressed In Modern Scientific Psychology. Web publication accessed in May 2014. http://www.soc.hawaii.edu/leonj/leonj/leonpsy/instructor/gloss.html

James Jakobovits, L. (1993). Swedenborg's religious psychology: The marriage of good and truth as mental health. *Studia Swedenborgiana*, 8(3), 13-42. Copy available here: Web document accessed in May 2014. http://www.soc.hawaii.edu/leonj/leonj/leonpsy/instructor/marriage/marrtext1to15.html

James, L. & Nahl, D. (1982) The coming Swedenborgian revolution in the social sciences and humanities. *Logos*. Winter 1982. Copy available here:

http://www.soc.hawaii.edu/leonj/499s98/shintani/logos.html Web document accessed in May 2014.

(13) Suzuki, D. T. (1996). *Swedenborg: Buddha of the North*. West Chester: Swedenborg Foundation. Reprinted on the Web at: http://ccbs.ntu.edu.tw/FULLTEXT/JR-PHIL/ew94208.htm

(14) Thompson, I. (2011). *Starting Science from God: Rational Scientific Theories from Theism*. Pleasanton: Eagle Pearl Press.
Sylvia, E. F. (2010). *Proving God: Swedenborg's Remarkable Quest for the Quantum Fingerprints of Love*. Staircase Press.

Baker, G. (2005). A dualistic model of ultimate reality and meaning: Self-similarity in chaotic dynamics and Swedenborg. The New Philosophy January-June 191-210.

(15) Bryntesson, F. (2009). The life cycle of the human immune-deficiency virus: A useful tool for teaching scientific and New Church principles in the biology Classroom. *The New Philosophy* January-June 761-790.

Shank, R. P. (2007). A tripartite theory of consciousness and mind: the neural-menton conjunction hypothesis. *The New Philosophy* January-June 7-33.

(16) Block, N., Flanagan, O. & Guzeldere, G. (Eds.). (1997). *The Nature of Consciousness: Philosophical Debates*. MIT Bradford Book.

(17) Damasio, A.R. (1994). *Descartes' Error: Emotion, Reason, and the Human Brain*. New York: Avon Books.

Johnson, M. (1987). *The Body in the Mind: The Bodily Basis of Meaning, Imagination, and Reason*. Chicago: University of Chicago Press.

(18) Damasio, A.R. (1994). *Descartes' Error: Emotion, Reason, and the Human Brain*. New York: Avon Books.

(19) Swedenborg, SE 5189; TCR 205

(20) Swedenborg, AC 1 and throughout the 12 volumes; WH 12; SS 9

(21) Swedenborg, AC throughout

(22) Thompson, I. (2011). *Starting Science from God: Rational Scientific Theories from Theism*. Pleasanton: Eagle Pearl Press.

(23) Tafel, R. L. (1890). *Documents Concerning the Life and Character of Emanuel Swedenborg*. London: Swedenborg Society. Copy available online at http://swedenborgdigitallibrary.org/tafel/tafeltc.html Accessed on the Web in May 2014.

(24) Swedenborg, DP 97
[25] Swedenborg, DLW 377; AC 3628
[26] Swedenborg, DP 73; AC 3043
[27] Swedenborg, DLW 205; SS 38; CL 314; TCR 214
[29] Swedenborg, DLW 179
[30] Swedenborg, DLW 99
[31] Swedenborg, DLW 69
[32] Swedenborg, TCR 30
[34] Swedenborg, AC 168
[35] Swedenborg, DLW 83

(36) James, L. (1995). Swedenborg Encyclopedia of Theistic Psychology. The Ideas of Emanuel Swedenborg (1668-1772) Expressed In Modern Scientific Psychology. Web publication accessed in May 2014.
http://www.soc.hawaii.edu/leonj/leonj/leonpsy/instructor/gloss.html

James Jakobovits, L. (1993). Swedenborg's religious psychology: The marriage of good and truth as mental health. *Studia Swedenborgiana*, 8(3), 13-42. Copy available here: (Web document accessed in May 2014)
http://www.soc.hawaii.edu/leonj/leonj/leonpsy/instructor/marriage/marrtext1to15.html

[37] Swedenborg, DLW 283, 82; TCR 76

[39] Swedenborg, DLW 324

[40] Swedenborg, ISB 11; DLW 251

[41] Swedenborg, DLW 1 and throughout

[43] Swedenborg, DP 51; AC 7381; DLW 155

[44] Swedenborg, TCR 33; DLW 302

[45] Swedenborg, DLW 77

[47] Swedenborg, DLW 277; TCR 565

[48] Swedenborg, DLW 212; DLW 165

[51] Swedenborg, SS 40

(52) Bigelow, J. (1912). *The Bible That Was Lost and is Found*. New York: New Church Board of Publication. Accessed on the Web in November 2014: https://archive.org/details/biblethatwaslos01bigegoog

(53) Hanegraaff, W. J. (2007). *Swedenborg, Oetinger, Kant: Three Perspectives on the Secrets of Heaven (Swedenborg Studies)*. Westchester, PA: Swedenborg Foundation Publishers.

(54) Hanegraaff, W. J. (2007). *Swedenborg, Oetinger, Kant: Three Perspectives on the Secrets of Heaven (Swedenborg Studies)*. Westchester, PA: Swedenborg Foundation Publishers.

(55) Hanegraaff, 2007, p.67.
Emerson, R.W. (1850). *Representative Men: Seven Lectures. Swedenborg or, the Mystic*. 1st World Library - Literary Society.

(56) Emerson, 1850

(57) James, L. (2004). *Principles of Theistic Psychology: The Scientific Knowledge of God Extracted from the Correspondential Sense of Sacred Scripture*. Web publication accessed in May 2014. http://e swedenborg.com/tp/books/theistic/index.htm

[58] Swedenborg, AC 1404, 1783

[59] James, L., 2004

(60) James, L. (2004b). Principles of Theistic Psychology. The Correspondential Meaning of Yoga Sayings and Asanas, of the Mudras in Buddhism, of Pranayama, and of the Bhagavad Gita. Chapter 10. Web document accessed in November 2014: http://www.soc.hawaii.edu/leonj/yoga.htm#hindi

[61] Swedenborg, SS 40

[62] New Testament, Matthew 13

[63] Swedenborg, AC 9138

[64] Swedenborg, AC 1540

(65) Silverman, Ray. (2011). Helen Keller: Seer of a New Civilization. Introduction to Helen Keller, *How I Would Help the World* (1904). West Chester, PA: Swedenborg Foundation Press.

(66) Keller, H. (1953). *My Religion*. New York: Swedenborg Foundation.

Death is psychologically as important as birth, and like it, is an integral part of life. ... As a doctor, I make every effort to strengthen the belief in immortality, especially with older patients when such questions come threateningly close. For, seen in correct psychological perspective, death is not an end but a goal, and life's inclination towards death begins as soon as the meridian is passed. ~Carl Jung, CW 13, Para. 68.

We ought to remember that the Fathers of the Church have insisted upon the fact that God has given Himself to man's death on the Cross so that we may become gods. ~Carl Jung, Letters Vol. II, Pages 312-316.

Chapter 2
Jung's Religiosity and Relationship to God

Jung's Spiritual Psychology and Swedenborg's Secret

When I've seen Jung's work being presented in general textbook-type summaries and reviews there was no indication or awareness of Jung's lifelong and deep relationship with God. Among modern day Freudians there is the belief that Jung had "an inconclusive position on religion", "an ambiguous treatment of religion", and "a view on religion within principally psychological perspective". (1) Jung himself has contributed to this appearance by the way he wrote about religion and God, and by the way he did not write about them.

Jung wrote about the principal Christian and other religious symbols in the context of analytic psychology. He wrote for instance about the "Trinity" and "quaternity" that "science ought not to treat them as anything other than "projections". Jung was persistent and unfailing in mentioning science in all his work. He felt more protected and safer when he erected the wall of science between himself and the revolutionary mind blowing ideas that Jung was putting forth to the Western intellect.

Having by his own report read seven volumes of Swedenborg's 27-volume set, Jung may have read Swedenborg's "Heavenly Secrets" about human development and depth psychology. There are several ways this subject is presented in Swedenborg. One is by means of the psychobiological principle that *individual mental development recapitulates evolution of history and civilization*. Another way to express this is the statement that the steps a person makes in the path to wholeness, self-realization, individuation, or regeneration recapitulate the steps by which the incarnated God-Man Christ regenerated and "glorified" the human physical body that He inherited from the Virgin Mary.

Regarding this "heavenly secret" about human development, Swedenborg makes a heroic attempt to prove its authenticity by writing 21 volumes of a collection of rational proofs through the analysis of the verses in the Old and New Testaments.

We may conclude either that Jung read Swedenborg's secrets, or else that he himself discovered some of them through his studies of universal religious symbolism and their relation to psychology and biology. Either way we can be sure that Jung was completely convinced that *religious symbols express specific mental activities in human development and in the evolution of civilization*. Jung understood that the function of religion is to bring individuals within the sphere of psychic reality.

It is clear that what Jung calls *individuation* and wholeness depend on the individual being willing to harness the negative psychic forces that are connected to the individual by birth or inheritance, and are *constantly active*

in preventing upward, inward, and positive development of the personality.
The hostile psychic forces that come into contact with our mind work to encourage the expression of inherited negative tendencies that human selfishness desires and loves.

The first step is getting to know their existence and actions in our mind. This requires self-examination of our thoughts, intentions, and delights.

Our thoughts and emotions that are harmful to others and to ourselves, are numerous, as for example:

- cursing people or wishing them ill because we don't like them
- wanting to deprive various people of their goods, to cheat them
- feeling elated at the misfortune of people's whom we don't favor
- contemplating and planning to cheat on agreements and laws
- feeling anxious and stressed, or depressed, unable to focus
- feeling restless and unable to work or be productive
- enjoying the idea of vengeance and mayhem, being cruel
- wanting to be served and honored by everyone, feeling superior
- acting hypocritically for gain and reputation, lying in relationships
- unable to maintain a long-term relationship or job
- practicing a materialist philosophy that opposes theism and dualism,
- intolerance and prejudice against those who are different, discriminatory
- incapacitating neuroses, obsessions, psychoses, split personality,
- personality disorders and character aberrations or perversions,
- harmful addictions, unhealthy lifestyles, lack of emotional intelligence,
- violent religious extremism, abuse of children and women,
- all mental, genetic, and physical dysfunctions and malformations,
- all viral infections in the body and harmful bacterial activity,
- etc.

Both Jung and Swedenborg attributed all human ills to the unconscious negative psychic forces that acted into people's minds, and from there into their bodies. Both writers held that the events in the natural world are all effects caused by events in the spiritual or mental world. Consciousness and meaning are primary spiritual features of the human mind. The mental world of eternity, which is the world of the collective unconscious in Jung's framework, is infinite and contains all that is possible for human beings to experience and to be conscious of. All truths and falsification of truths are contained in the collective unconscious or mental world of eternity.

Truths and falsified truths are spiritual causes of natural events. A viral infection or an earthquake are events in the natural world that are effects of spiritual or mental causes. Falsification of truths and selfish loves are spiritual events in the mental world that have the power to cause negative and harmful effects in the natural world. Truths in the mental world have the power to cause positive and useful events in the natural world, such as sunshine, animal instincts, birthday celebrations, or healing herbs. The relation between specific natural events as being effects, such as rain, horses, gold, locusts, bees, etc., and specific mental events as being their causes, has been explored and described by Swedenborg under the subject of "correspondences". (2)

Jung recommended to his patients to practice the method of "active imagination" through which one faces the scary psychic forces of the collective unconscious. He discovered this method when he for several years felt the compulsion to face those negative psychic forces. He describes his mental struggles in *The Red Book* where he tells about various psychic or mental characters that confronted Jung. *He realizes eventually when he is near victory that those characters are the parts of him, the parts that he has not yet been able to integrate into his development.*

Gradually over his long writing career Jung was able to present a coherent psychological theory of how mental health and disorder operate simultaneously in two distinct realms or worlds in which every patient lives. The ordinary everyday consciousness by which people do their work and maintain a social life, is a materialistic consciousness, such as Freud promoted throughout his life and career as a mental health practitioner. The work of Jung and Swedenborg develop the thesis that mental health disorders and dysfunctions plaguing people's materialistic consciousness cannot be permanently eradicated using materialistic methods alone, as Freud was doing. The cause of the dysfunction is in the psychic world, and so is the solution.

Jung's Incompatibility With Freud

Freud and Jung have put exactly opposite pressures on the development of psychology as a science. Freud continued the erroneous trend in psychology of eliminating the psychic world as a dimension of reality in its own sphere. *Freud reduced the human mind to the chemistry of the brain.* He fought the spiritual like a demon and tried to eliminate it from existence. He ridiculed religion as mere superstition and belittled those who put God into their lives as the childish need for a "father figure". Freud thus had no respect or feeling for the spiritual in humanity, its hopes, its prayers, its striving to rise above the animal level. Freud's atheistic psychology was therefore a menace to society and community. This conclusion is of course not shared by followers of Freud who continue to function in the context of materialistic psychology.

From the perspective of Freudians the religiosity of Jung is seen as a lifelong unresolved "*psychological complex left over from Jung's difficult childhood stemming from his deep conflict with his preacher father's personality*". This type of reductionist Freudian perspective functions to obscure the rational understanding regarding all issues of religion in connection with Jung. One wonders how it was even possible for Jung to collaborate and work with Freud at the beginning of Jung's professional career. Decades later Jung confesses that he had to suppress himself in the presence of Freud in order to keep working with him:

> *Under the impress of Freud's personality I had, as far as possible, cast aside my own judgments and repressed my criticisms. That was the prerequisite for collaborating with him. (Jung, Memories, Dreams, Reflections, 1962)*

The figure below summarizes the results of a contrastive study I made of the overlap in key topics in the collected works of Freud, Jung, and Swedenborg. (3)

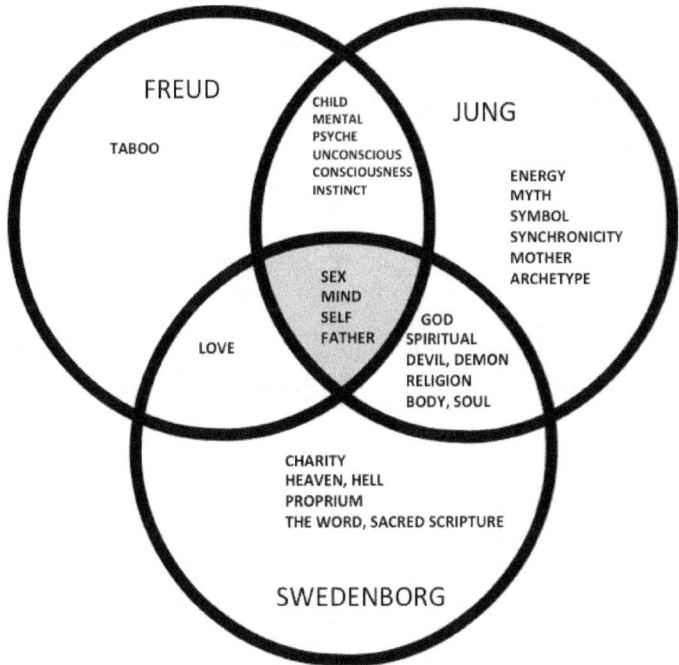

FREUD

JUNG

TABOO

CHILD
MENTAL
PSYCHE
UNCONSCIOUS
CONSCIOUSNESS
INSTINCT

ENERGY
MYTH
SYMBOL
SYNCHRONICITY
MOTHER
ARCHETYPE

SEX
MIND
SELF
FATHER

GOD
SPIRITUAL
DEVIL, DEMON
RELIGION
BODY, SOUL

LOVE

CHARITY
HEAVEN, HELL
PROPRIUM
THE WORD, SACRED SCRIPTURE

SWEDENBORG

Jung's familiarity and involvement with the "spiritualistic" literature is clearly exhibited in his voluminous citations throughout his books and articles, and in the titles of some of his important works, such as, "On Spiritualistic Phenomena" (1905), "The Archetypes and the Collective Unconscious" (1981), and "Psychology of Alchemy" (1944), "The Spirit in Man" (1978), "A Psychological Approach To The Trinity" (Collected Works, V.11), "The Soul and Death" (1934), "The Psychological Foundations of Belief in Spirits" (1920).

> The collective unconscious - so far as we can say anything about it at all - appears to consist of mythological motifs or primordial images, for which reason the myths of all nations are its real exponents. In fact, the whole of mythology could be taken as a sort of projection of the collective unconscious... We can therefore study the collective unconscious in two ways, either in mythology or in the analysis of the individual. (Jung, The Structure of the Psyche, CW 8, par. 325.)

Jung was intensely interested in characterizing the movement of objects or meanings in the non-spatial psychic world of the collective unconscious. He discovered that traveling around in the world of the collective unconscious is very different from travel with the material mental content of the ordinary individual conscious through imagination and memory. It is shown below that this is precisely the relationship that Swedenborg intensely examined and called the "correspondences" between collective and individual consciousness. Jung formulated the concept of synchronicity in order to study the connection between the two worlds. The psychic world is immaterial and purely mental or spiritual, thus apart from the limits imposed by physical time and space. The natural world is material and thus leads to natural consciousness, which is based in sensory input from the physical world and in abstractions derived from these.

Freud revolutionized people's idea of the self and uncovered new motivational layers underneath the individual's surface or visible personality. He wrote about the unconscious from what he could discern from his material consciousness, and as a result all of Freud's concepts of the psyche consist exclusively of material cognitions. He never allowed himself to penetrate, as Jung and Swedenborg did, below the natural surface into another degree of depth, another realm of existence. As a result all his ideas and principles about human beings were flattened into a single mode of material existence known in the history of psychology as monism, to distinguish the attitude from dualism. Freud's ideas of the psyche, the individual unconscious, or the libido were reduced into a material dimension, equating mind and its consciousness with the neuro-chemistry of the brain and the physics of mechanics.

Freud upheld the strict methodology of materialistic science as it appeared to him at the beginning of the twentieth century. It is a historical irony that after Freud's death psychology in the second half of the twentieth century turned towards behaviorism so that Freud's work was often ridiculed as unscientific and filled with concepts that had no empirical measurement status. This rejection did not affect the loyalty of Freudians for the ideas and methods of psychoanalysis. Today Freud is still one of the most cited names in psychology and psychiatry.

Freud referred to the "powerful mental dynamics" that is always ongoing in the individual unconscious. These intense psychic energies include repression and resistance to analysis in therapy. Psychoanalysis is a method by which this unconscious resistance can be counteracted and neutralized so that the idea that was repressed can now become conscious and dealt with practically in behavior.

Nevertheless Freud maintained that the conscious and unconscious are not in a continuous degree of less to more clearness of view, but in discrete degrees so that the two are dichotomous, either one, or the other (p. 3950). He warned that "we must beware of ignoring this [discrete] characteristic, for the property of being conscious or not is in the last resort our one beacon-light in the darkness of depth-psychology" (Freud, *Collected Works*, p. 3951).

In contrast to Freud's monism, Jung's dualism recognized in prayer and religion a psychic relationship that was real and powerful. Sometimes Jung talked as if it was the collective unconscious that should be considered God. He endowed the collective unconscious with creative powers. *Jung's dualist topics of "synchronicity" and "archetype" do not occur anywhere in Freud's Collected Works!* It was impossible for Freud to see dualism as other than superstition or useless idealism. Although the word God appears 837 times in the *Collected Works* of Freud, the references were derogatory and hostile, as shown by these statements:

> *I have tried to show that religious ideas have arisen from the same need as have all the other achievements of civilization: from the necessity of defending oneself against the crushingly superior force of nature. To this a second motive was added - the urge to rectify the shortcomings of civilization which made themselves painfully felt. (Freud, Collected Works p. 4433)*

> *I believe that a large part of the mythological view of the world, which extends a long way into the most modern religions, is nothing but psychology projected into the external world. The obscure recognition (the endopsychic perception, as it were) of psychical factors and relations in the unconscious is mirrored - it is difficult to express it in other terms, and here the analogy with paranoia must come to our aid - in the construction of a supernatural reality, which is destined to be changed back once more by science into the psychology of the unconscious. One could venture to explain in this way the myths of paradise and the fall of man, of God, of good and evil, of immortality, and so on, and to transform metaphysics into metapsychology. The gap between the paranoic's displacement and that of the superstitious person is*

less wide than it appears at first sight. (Freud, *The Psychopathology Of Everyday Life*, p. 1328)

At first the concept of the unconscious was limited to denoting the state of repressed or forgotten contents. Even with Freud, who makes the unconscious-at least metaphorically ¬take the stage as the acting subject, it is really nothing but the gathering place of forgotten and repressed contents, and has a functional significance thanks only to these. For Freud, accordingly, the unconscious is of an exclusively personal nature, although he was aware of its archaic and mythological thought-forms.

A more or less superficial layer of the unconscious is undoubtedly personal. I call it the personal unconscious. But this personal unconscious rests upon a deeper layer, which does not derive from personal experience and is not a personal acquisition but is inborn. This deeper layer I call the collective unconscious. I have chosen the term "collective" because this part of the unconscious is not individual but universal; in contrast to the personal psyche, it has contents and modes of behaviour that are more or less the same everywhere and in all individuals. It is, in other words, identical in all men and thus constitutes a common psychic substrate of a suprapersonal nature which is present in everyone of us.

Psychic existence can be recognized only by the presence of contents that are capable of consciousness. We can therefore speak of an unconscious only in so far as we are able to demonstrate its contents. The contents of the personal unconscious are chiefly the feeling-toned complexes, as they are called; they constitute the personal and private side of psychic life. The contents of the collective unconscious, on the other hand, are known as archetypes. (Jung, *Archetypes and the Collective Unconscious*, 1934, 3)

> Footnote 2: In his later works Freud differentiated the basic view mentioned here. He called the instinctual psyche the "id," and his "super-ego" denotes the collective consciousness, of which the individual is partly conscious and partly unconscious (because it is repressed).

Given Freud's materialism and atheism it was inevitable that he would come to think of God as a dependency pathology similar to that involved in a "paranoic's displacement". God is nothing but "psychology projected outward". It may be that Freud had the direction wrong, unlike Jung and

Swedenborg who knew that God and the unconscious were inward of the person, hence reaching for God was to go inward, and not as Freud thought of projecting something outward from one's personality or wishes.

> It must be remembered, too, that the belief in spirits and ghosts and the return of the dead, which finds so much support in the religions to which we have all been attached, at least in our childhood, is far from having disappeared among educated people, and that many who are sensible in other respects find it possible to combine spiritualism with reason. A man who has grown rational and skeptical, even, may be ashamed to discover how easily he may for a moment return to a belief in spirits under the combined impact of strong emotion and perplexity. (Freud, Delusions And Dreams In Jensen's Gradiva, p. 1865)

To Freud a "belief in spirits" is abnormal and he wonders that "many who are sensible in other respects find it possible to combine spiritualism with reason". We don't know all that Freud means here when denigrating the idea of "spiritualism", but if one considers the contributions to depth psychology of Jung and Swedenborg, we can see how Freud's materialism flattens and weakens his own understanding of basic human behavior.

My study of the contrast between Freud, Jung, and Swedenborg led me to the following conclusions summarized in this table:

	Freud 1856–1939	Jung 1875 -1961	Swedenborg 1688-1772
Type of explanations	Physical, neural, sensorimotor	Rational, symbolic, collective	Rational, correspondential, collective
Philosophy of science	Materialistic monism	Psychic dualism	Anatomical substantive dualism
Intense topic focus	Child, mind, instinct, ego-self, father, sex	Consciousness, unconscious, ego-self, symbol, mind	Psychic societies, correspondences, spiritual love, evils of selfishness, spiritual adulteration
Discoveries	The individual unconscious	The collective unconscious	The collective conscious
Idea of God	Atheistic	Personal theistic	Collective theistic
Use of special vocabulary	Taboo, fixation, conversion, libido, psychoanalysis, repression sublimation	Archetype, collective unconscious, hidden symbol, complexes, individuation	Correspondences, spiritual societies, regeneration, vastation, discrete levels, proprium, conjugial love, scortatory insanities

Freud's philosophy of science may be called "materialistic monism". He was a passionate atheist, viewing religion and God as fabrications of people's childish need for a "father figure". Freud defined consciousness in reductionist terms using physics and biology to describe psychodynamic operations. From that perspective it was impossible for him to see anything real in what was not part of the material structure of the body and world. Jung on the other hand was able to escape the material consciousness of the body senses. His focus on individuation and self-realization allowed Jung to become aware of the existence of a psychic or mental world that is distinct from the physical world. Jung's philosophy may therefore be called *psychic dualism*, as exemplified by his concept of the "archetype", a word that does not appear in all of Freud's Collected Works.

It seems impossible for anyone seeing Jung from the Freudian perspective, to understand Jung's spiritual psychotherapy, whose theme he summarized in Latin as *Spiritus contra spiritum*, that is, fighting the spirit with the spirit (discussed in Chapter 1 above):

> "Alcohol in Latin is "spiritus" and you use the same word for the highest religious experience as well as for the most depraving poison. The helpful formula therefore is: spiritus contra spiritum."

Jung was talking about the hopelessness of psychotherapy for one of his patients who was killing himself with alcohol and had arrived at his final phase. Jung knew that it was the negative psychic forces ("spiritum") that are killing him. The only hope left he thought was "spiritus" or God. In the letter Jung talked about the need for a "religious conversion" experience to break the hold of the negative spirits. Thirty years later Jung received an unexpected letter that confirmed his insight.

To understand Jung's important insight it is necessary to be a dualist like Jung and Swedenborg. As a dualist one can think that the psychic forces are real and exist in the psychic world in which our mind exists. The highest religious experience Jung was referring to is "union" or "conjunction" with God. Many believe that union with God refers to an ecstatic experience that lasts for a short while and then is left in our memory. However it is doubtful that this is the sense that Jung was indicating. There is no history in his writings of a focus on such an experience. Instead he often discusses the experience of the "numinous" as facing the archetypes of the collective unconscious. But conjunction with God was a daily philosophy and an ordinary event, normal like breathing and eating:

> *Besides this world there existed another realm, like a temple in which anyone who entered was transformed and suddenly overpowered by a vision of the whole cosmos, so that he could only marvel and admire, forgetful of himself. Here lived the "Other," who knew God as a hidden, personal, and at the same time supra-personal secret. Here nothing separated man from God; indeed, it*

was as though the human mind looked down upon Creation simultaneously with God. (Jung, Memories, 62)

Swedenborg described union with God as conjunction by reciprocation. Again, this is not an extraordinary event of transpersonal ecstasy but a way of dealing with daily ordinary life. Swedenborg explains that God's purpose in creating the universe was to create individual human beings who could acknowledge God as the Creator and manager of life. This acknowledgement is the reciprocation that God desires because it allows God to elevate the individual into a life of wholeness and eternal happiness. The physical universe and all its contents have been created for the sole purpose of meeting this Divine end.

Religious Topics in Jung

Jung may be considered an expert on the psychology of the Christian religion. He was brought up in that religion and culture, and has had a lifelong involvement in understanding the inner meaning and symbolism of all of religion, which he understood to be the repository of the human archetypes.

What Jung called the unfathomable deep collective unconscious, Swedenborg called the spiritual world of the afterlife of humanity. That great deep unconscious becomes conscious when we undergo the two-day dying-resuscitation process and cross into the afterlife of eternity. *Death turns the collective unconscious into the collective conscious.* Every individual is resuscitated within 48 hours and awakens in the spiritual body, no longer in sensory contact with the physical world. Spiritual consciousness is then the ordinary everyday method of functioning.

Spiritual language is inborn and universal, and remains unconscious until resuscitation. Many other new mental functions are then experienced such as instant teleportation or telepathy. When we join one of the many psychic societies in the afterlife we discover that our thoughts and emotions are no longer private and individual. There is a sharing of inner mental states to the entire society, each receiving what the other has. This is the *collective conscious*. This sharing provides a constant enrichment of one's loves and interests. Those who have thoughts and emotions that are incompatible with the others feel themselves expelled as it were, and they find themselves in another psychic society that is more similar to them.

In the *Collected Works* Jung mentions Swedenborg in two connections. One is a story about Swedenborg that was widely circulated at the time. Jung was aware of Kant's interest and later rejection of Swedenborg's theology and dual consciousness. The story that got Kant interested in Swedenborg is the same as what caught Jung's interest. This story is not mentioned anywhere in Swedenborg's Writings and Swedenborg did not write an autobiography. The story is that Swedenborg was at dinner with various people of note in Swedish society. This was at a location 500 miles from Stockholm where his house was located. Swedenborg got very agitated for several minutes reporting that a fire in that city block was threatening his house and he had valuable manuscripts that he must not loose. But after a few minutes he calmed down saying that the fire had been extinguished before it got to his house. The next day couriers came from Stockholm and told the news about Baron Swedenborg's house and how the fire at first spread then was contained. Also the time when it happened.

This clairvoyance story was retold by various people who were present as evidenced by letters that are still extant today. Jung was quite interested in such evidence and was a keen reader of William James who discussed this topic from an academic and psychological perspective. The possibility of such an event greatly impressed Jung, along with other parapsychological phenomena he looked into such as automatic writing and reading one's future as in the I Ching. To Jung such events proved that there is another realm that has different laws and limits than the physical world. It was the beginning of Jung's psychic dualism, the idea that the human unconscious is a collective unconscious not merely individual! The collective unconscious is another world that has powerful influences on this world. To merely study this natural world, as Freud did, could not give a practical understanding of human psychology.

The second topic that Jung mentions about Swedenborg is the "*Maximus Homo*" or Grand Man. This is the idea in Swedenborg's Writings that since God is Divine Human and the original infinite human, everything created necessarily reflects in some measure the image and likeness of the human form. The human body and its many internal anatomical structures is an outward visible image of the interior spiritual body, which is the mind. The human mind, when visible, looks like the body and its inner and outer parts. Furthermore, to God the whole human race looks unified as one human being. This is the Grand Man or Homo Maximus that Jung briefly alludes to several times in his articles and books. Especially is this striking as Swedenborg was allowed on a few occasions to actually see this collective or composite form from a distance as it were, and he reports that the Grand Man looks like a well-formed handsome human being that possesses the organs of both sexes.

And still further, The Grand Man or Grand Human is composed of numberless spiritual societies gathered together each according to shared loves and interests. All these societies are unified by each society having a unique identifying interest and aptitude. Swedenborg travelled through this human mental space in eternity for 27 years on a daily basis through his dual consciousness. He had studied human anatomy for several years prior to this experience and wrote several books on it. (2)

Swedenborg made the striking discovery that the identifying character of each society was related by correspondence to the physiological function of the anatomical part in which that particular society lived in the Grand Human. For example, the psychic societies that occupied the region of the stomach were involved in inducing anxiety feelings in the stomach to people on earth who were psychologically connected to those particular societies. This evidence must have amazed Jung, assuming he was aware of it. Like many others exposed to Swedenborg's Writings he had to make up his mind whether this was real or made up. Here is an instance of how Swedenborg presents this discovery.

THOSE WHO RELATE TO THE STOMACH.

Many anxieties appear to have their seat in the stomach, and the influx of such [anxiety-producing] spirits is felt there, and sometimes the anxieties [appear] to be there, like those of avarice, which are numerous. Such anxieties, when the persons distress themselves because they have to part with their money, appear to dwell in that organ. There are also other anxieties, which, likewise, are plainly perceived in the stomach; some inwardly, some higher, and some lower, according to the difference between them. I often talked with the spirits who induced [the sensations], and who are in the province of the stomach. They correspond to indigestion, and hence to the sense of oppression.

Moreover, the stomach corresponds to the desire of knowing for the sake of use, thus of digesting and appropriating those things which are tributary to use. Then is the stomach in its freedom, and expands freely, and the lungs operate freely upon it; hence, also, life is delightful. In the other case, it is restricted, nor is it able to attain to freedom. There were certain ones with me above the head, for some hours. I did not observe their presence from anything else than a certain anxious feeling, of which one becomes aware in the lower part of the stomach. Hence, it was evident that they had communication with such as infested the stomach, and those who had their province there. I spoke with the same; and I said that I wished they would retire, because they do not accord with the sphere of those spirits who are with me: for they are repugnant to it.

Then, also, there was conversation about spheres, [to the effect] that there are very many such spheres around men, and that they do not observe that there are; and that many, likewise, produce their effect, like those effects are produced which arise from exhalations, and from repugnance at any one's presence, from joy and freedom, and very many other things; so that spheres operate with men also: but, because they deny all that they do not see and feel in the body, and ascribe anything that appears occult, to nature, and scarcely anyone [believes] that such a thing is from the spiritual world - owing to all this, they reflect little upon it; and they who do reflect, put it aside either as a recondite natural [phenomenon], or as nothing, because they do not understand it. (Swedenborg, Spiritual Experiences Minor, n. 4789)

One can see Jung's fascination with this idea, being a therapist all his life and had to deal with neuroses and anxieties in his patients. Freud would have rejected Swedenborg's account as insane. Freud is like the materialist thinker mentioned in the last sentence above who hears about the account then puts it aside as nothing. Such also was Kant's public judgment of Swedenborg's claims. If Jung had been a Swedenborgian psychologist he would have clearly seen the relationship between his patients' neurotic physical symptoms and the corresponding mental causes from the power of the archetypes. Jung would have realized more clearly that it is the archetypes that cause the symptoms in the physical body. What

Swedenborg observed to be the location of the spirits in the Grand Human is their archetype.

Each spiritual society is uniquely located in some anatomical part of the Grand Human. Each society's logo or distinguishing mark on this anatomical map is an archetype. There are as many archetypes in the spiritual world, and hence in the collective unconscious, as there are spiritual or psychic communities there, and Swedenborg reports that they are numberless, given that they contain in totality all human beings that were ever born on some planet and passed on into the world of eternity since the beginning of the universe.

Jung was attracted to these two features of Swedenborg, namely, his clairvoyance and his idea of the Grand Human. It appears that Jung was probably not aware of the relationship between the place in the Maximus Homo and neurotic symptoms he was treating. Nor was Jung certain of the idea that the collective unconscious is where people "went" when passing on. Nor was Jung aware that archetypes were spiritual forces originating in spiritual societies that were in unconscious contact with the patients, and indeed, with every human being. Had Jung been aware of these items in Swedenborg he would have discussed them, as he did those two items of which he was aware.

But it's also possible that Swedenborg was outside the limits of Jung's professional ability to discuss other worldly topics from the perspective of a mental travelogue by a philosopher and "mystic" who claimed to live in dual consciousness. This was also Kant's problem, who in a letter asked a friend not to mention that Kant had purchased some Swedenborg books as this might injure his chances of obtaining a professorship in analytical philosophy for which he was being considered at the time in a German university. (4). Similarly, this may have inhibited William James of ever mentioning in public Swedenborg's ideas, given that James was making a claim with his books of helping to lay down the principles of a new modern empirical psychology.

William James had earlier edited for a posthumous publication his father Henry James' notes on Swedenborg, which were quite voluminous. (5) And throughout his upbringing William was exposed to his father's proselytizing enthusiasm for Swedenborg for many years.   And yet the name Swedenborg cannot be found in James' famous book *Varieties of Religious*

Experiences, (6), nor in his influential book *Principles of Psychology* (6). Kant, William James, Jung, and perhaps other scientists and academicians could have been discouraged of citing anything by Swedenborg due to the risk to their scientific reputation.

For instance, Jung states in his presentation at the prestigious Terry Lectures that he was invited to give at Yale University in 1937:

> *Although I have often been called a philosopher, I am an empiricist and adhere as such to the phenomenological standpoint. I trust that it does not conflict with the principles of scientific empiricism if one occasionally makes certain reflections which go beyond a mere accumulation and classification of experience. ... I approach psychological matters from a scientific and not from a philosophical standpoint. Inasmuch as religion has a very important psychological aspect, I deal with it from a purely empirical point of view, that is, I restrict myself to the observation of phenomena and I eschew any metaphysical or philosophical considerations. I do not deny the validity of these other considerations, but I cannot claim to be competent to apply them correctly.*

Compare Jung's cautious, perhaps timid, attitude about dualism with Swedenborg's direct and self-assured eyewitness ethnography. Swedenborg writes:

> [Note: "spirits and angels" refer to people who have passed on and live in the afterlife of eternity]

> *As regards spirits and angels in general, who all are human souls living after the death of the body, I may say here that they have much more exquisite senses than men-that is, sight, hearing, smell, and touch-but not taste. Spirits however are not able, and angels are still less able, to see anything that is in the world by their own sight, that is, by the sight of the spirit; for the light of the world or of the sun is to them as thick darkness; just in the same way as man by his sight, that is, by the sight of the body, cannot see anything that is in the other life; for the light of heaven, or the Lord's heavenly light, is to man as thick darkness.*

> *But still when the Lord pleases, spirits and angels can see the things in this world through the eyes of a man. But the Lord does not grant this except in the case of one whom He enables to speak with spirits and angels, and to*

be together with them. Spirits and angels have been permitted to see the things in this world through my eyes as plainly as I could see them myself, and also to hear men talking with me. It has sometimes happened that to their great astonishment, some through me have seen their friends whom they had had in the life of the body, just as they had seen them before. Some have also seen their married partners, and their children, and have desired me to tell them that they were close by and saw them, and to give an account of their state in the other life, but I had been forbidden to tell them or reveal to them that they were seen in this way, and this partly for the reason that they would have called me insane, or would have thought such things to be delirious fancies of the mind; for I was well aware that although they would acknowledge it with the lips, they did not believe in heart in the existence of spirits, or that the dead are risen.

When my interior sight was first opened, and through my eyes spirits and angels saw the world and the things that are in it, they were so amazed that they called it the miracle of miracles; and they were affected with a new joy, in that in this way communication was opened of earth with heaven, and of heaven with earth. This delight lasted for months, but afterwards it became familiar, and now they do not wonder at all. I have been instructed that the spirits and angels who are present with other men do not in the slightest degree see the things of this world, but only perceive the thoughts and affections of those with whom they are.

These things have shown that man was so created that while living on earth among men, he might at the same time also live in heaven among angels, and the converse; so that heaven and earth might be together, and might act as a one, and that men might know what is going on in heaven, and angels what in the world; and therefore that when men depart this life they would pass from the Lord's kingdom on earth into the Lord's kingdom in the heavens, not as into another kingdom, but as into the same as that in which they had been when living in the body. But in consequence of man's becoming so corporeal, he has closed heaven against himself. (n. 1880)

Spirits are exceedingly indignant, indeed are angry, when told that men do not believe that they see, that they hear, that they feel by the touch. They have said that surely men ought to know that without sense there is no life, and that the more exquisite the sense the more excellent the life; also that the objects of their sense are suited to the excellence of their senses, and that the representatives which are from the Lord are real, for all the things that are in nature and the world are derived from them (see n. 1632). The words in which they express their indignation are that they perceive by the senses much better and more excellently than men do. (Swedenborg, *Secrets of Heaven*, AC 1880)

Swedenborg was well aware of the impossibility of the material mind to accept his eyewitness reports as real, which is the reason he did not talk about it to many people, as he says above, "*partly for the reason that they would have called me insane, or would have thought such things to be delirious fancies of the mind*". I am assuming that that is what Kant, Jung, and William James were afraid of when they refrained from mentioning Swedenborg in their articles, lectures, and books. Jung goes as far as to say that he is not studying religion as a phenomenon but rather the psychology of the religious man. Jung thus shifts his topic away from religion and restricts himself to the person who acts from religion.

As I am a doctor and a specialist in nervous and mental diseases, my point of departure is not a creed but the psychology of the homo religiosus, the man who takes into account and carefully observes certain factors which influence him and, through him, his general condition. (Jung, *Psychology and Religion*, p. 12)

In his pioneering book *The Varieties of Religious Experience* William James introduced the same distinction between religion itself and the religious person in order, I believe, to protect his reputation as an empiricist in the new modern scientific psychology that he was helping to establish. This focus distinction has remained for over a century now. For instance the American Psychological Association has for decades sponsored a professional interest Group called The Psychological Study of Religion, which however in fact is the study, not of religion, but of religious behavior and attitudes. Swedenborg on the other hand deals with religion and its ideas as a reality for science, as well as with God's relationship to human beings, including their salvation through cessation of "sinning" and the consequent regeneration of their hellish character to heavenly.

"Sinning" refers to all behaviors and attitudes that are motivated by selfishness or "the love of self for the sake of self". The healed personality is that of loving others as much as self. This positive altruistic motive effectively represses the self-centered habits that spurn cruelty, deception, and prejudice. Swedenborg realized that the selfish "unregenerate" personality is destructive of community life and changes positive spiritual evolution to negative devolution of the human condition. One leads to a personality that can subsist and develop in heavenly communities, while the other leads to a negative and insane personality that devolves into a life of hell and community degradation.

It is significant that Jung had a Latin inscription carved in stone above the door of his house in Switzerland. It said: "*vocatus atque non vocatus deus aderit*, i.e., "Called or not called, the god will be there." There is a picture of it on the Web at: http://www.jungnewyork.com/photo_vocatus.shtml). Jung explains the inscription in a letter:

> *By the way, you seek the enigmatic oracle Vocatus atque non vocatus deus aderit in vain in Delphi: it is cut in stone over the door of my house in Kusnacht near Zurich and otherwise found in Erasmus's collection of Adagia (XVIth cent.). It is a Delphic oracle though. It says: yes, the god will be on the spot, but in what form and to what purpose? I have put the inscription there to remind my patients and myself: Timor dei initium sapiente ["The fear of the Lord is the beginning of wisdom."] Here another not less important road begins, not the approach to "Christianity" but to God himself and this seems to be the ultimate question. (Jung, Letters,1975: 611)*

Here is the photograph of Jung's inscription carved in stone above the door of his house in Switzerland.

107

God as a Personal Secret

God was for Jung "*the ultimate question*". The public inscription carved in stone above his front door is another instance of Jung's little recognized religiosity. The reminder was for "*my patients and myself*" that "*the fear of the Lord is the beginning of wisdom*". This quote appears twice in the Bible. One is *Proverb 9:9,10*:

> *Give instruction to a wise man and he will be still wiser, Teach a righteous man and he will increase his learning. The fear of the LORD is the beginning of wisdom, And the knowledge of the Holy One is understanding.*

The other is in Psalm 111:9,10:

> *He has sent redemption to His people; He has ordained His covenant forever; Holy and awesome is His name. The fear of the LORD is the beginning of wisdom; A good understanding have all those who do His commandments; His praise endures forever.*

Perhaps Jung felt safe disclosing his religiosity in public this way because it was not in print and because it was in Latin. How many of his patients or visitors could read Latin? Jung kept his deep relationship to God hidden from view until the very end of his life when he discloses it in his dictated autobiography, which he arranged to have published only after his death. In the following passage in his autobiography Jung talks about his relationship to God and the Christian Church of his parents when he was a schoolboy. In it he discloses his lifelong sense that he was composed of two different, contrastive, and opposing personalities.

> *Naturally I compensated my inner insecurity by an outward show of security, or--to put it better--the defect compensated itself without the intervention of my will. That is, I found myself being guilty and at the same time wishing to be innocent. Somewhere deep in the background I always knew that I was two persons. One was the son of my parents, who went to school and was less intelligent, attentive, hard-working, decent, and clean than many other boys. The other was grown up--old, in fact--skeptical, mistrustful, remote from the world of men, but close to nature, the earth, the sun, the moon, the weather, a living creatures, and above all close to the night, to dreams, and to whatever "God" worked directly in him. I put "God" in quotation marks here. For nature*

seemed, like myself, to have been set aside by God as non-divine, although created by Him as an expression of Himself.

Nothing could persuade me that "in the image of God" applied only to man. In fact it seemed to me that the high mountains, the rivers, lakes, trees, flowers, and animals far better exemplified the essence of God than men with their ridiculous clothes, their meanness, vanity, mendacity, and abhorrent egotism-- all qualities with which I was only too familiar from myself, that is, from personality No. 1, the schoolboy of 1890.

Besides this world there existed another realm, like a temple in which anyone who entered was transformed and suddenly overpowered by a vision of the whole cosmos, so that he could only marvel and admire, forgetful of himself. Here lived the "Other," who knew God as a hidden, personal, and at the same time supra-personal secret. Here nothing separated man from God; indeed, it was as though the human mind looked down upon Creation simultaneously with God. (Jung, Memories, 62)

This may be Jung's most revealing confession in his autobiography, giving us deep insight into his inner personality or self. Jung for the first time is able to bring himself to disclose that all his life he has managed two personalities of himself, being as he says "*two persons*". One of his personalities was the social outward face and character that was needed for society and his career as citizen, psychiatrist, and scientist. This is what he called "*the guilty part*" of himself. Jung's other personality was his inward face and character that saw his relationship to God as the central feature of his entire existence. Here he was "*close to nature*" and "*above all close to the night, to dreams, and to whatever "God" worked directly in him*". This was the "*innocent*" part of himself.

Even as a young boy Jung was able to see through the hypocritical religion of his parents and community. He realized this by witnessing the people's dishonesty and wickedness towards one another, "*with their ridiculous clothes, their meanness, vanity, mendacity, and abhorrent egotism--all qualities with which I was only too familiar from myself, that is, from personality No. 1, the schoolboy of 1890*". Jung had the insight of seeing himself as part of the social charade. But he was saved by his ability to acknowledge a dual world: "*Besides his world* [schoolboy Personality 1] *there existed another realm, like a temple in which anyone who entered was transformed and suddenly overpowered by a vision of the whole cosmos, so that he could only marvel and admire, forgetful of himself."* With triumph Jung declares: *"Here lived the "Other," [schoolboy Personality 2] who knew God as a hidden, personal, and at the same time supra-personal secret."*

Jung explains that his two personalities are mythical and universal. All people are structured that way though they don't normally know it:

> *... The play and counter play between personalities No. 1 and No. 2, which has run through my whole life, has nothing to do with a "split" or dissociation in the ordinary medical sense. On the contrary, it is played out in every individual. In my life No. 2 has been of prime importance and I have always tried to make room for anything that wanted to come to me from within. He is a typical figure, but he is perceived only by the very few. Most people's conscious understanding is not sufficient to realize that he is also what they are.*

Jung's precocious spiritual insights made it impossible for him to continue attending his parents' Church. His sincere inner relationship to God was scandalized by the blasphemy of what was going on in Church, namely, the profanation of innocent and *"inexpressible feelings"* with *"stale sentimentalities"*.

> *Church gradually became a place of torment to me. For there men dared to preach aloud--I am tempted to say, shamelessly—about God, about His intentions and actions. There people were exhorted to have those feelings and to believe that secret which I knew to be the deepest, innermost certainty, a certainty not to be betrayed by a single word. I could only conclude that apparently no one knew about this secret, not even the parson, for otherwise no one would have dared to expose the mystery of God in public and to profane those inexpressible feelings with stale sentimentalities.*

> *Moreover, I was certain that this was the wrong way to reach God, for I knew, knew from experience, that this grace was accorded only to one who fulfilled the will of God without reservation. This was preached from the pulpit, too, but always on the assumption that revelation had made the will of God plain. To me, on the other hand, it seemed the most obscure and unknown thing of all. To me it seemed that one's duty was to explore daily the will of God. I did not do that, but I felt sure that I would do it as soon as an urgent reason for so doing presented itself. Personality No. 1 preoccupied*

me too much of the time. It often seemed to me that religious precepts were being put in place of the will of God--which could be so unexpected and so alarming--for the sole purpose of sparing people the necessity for understanding God's will.

I grew more and more skeptical, and my father's sermons and those of other parsons became acutely embarrassing to me. All the people about me seemed to take the jargon for granted, and the dense obscurity that emanated from it; thoughtlessly they swallowed all the contradictions, such as that God is omniscient and therefore foresaw all human history, and that he actually created human beings so that they would have to sin, and nevertheless forbids them to sin and even punishes them by eternal damnation in hell-fire. (Jung, Memories, 63)

To Jung's young innocent mind it was revealed from within that doing God's will is required by religion: "*I knew, knew from experience, that this grace was accorded only to one who fulfilled the will of God without reservation*". The worship he saw in Church was "the wrong way to reach God". He therefore knew the spiritual truth of salvation: "*To me it seemed that one's duty was to explore daily the will of God*". Being honest and innocent Jung confesses: "*I did not do that, but I felt sure that I would do it as soon as an urgent reason for so doing presented itself.*" I'm not sure what Jung meant to say here. He may have been referring to the mental state of temptation in his daily life when struggling against a temptation to be selfish and dishonest. Perhaps the "urgent reason" would be the battle to death within him between Personality 1 and Personality 2.

Note here how Jung as a teenager was led to acknowledge God with sincerity of heart. He accepts the innocent thinking that God's commandments must be obeyed. As a young boy he started hating to go to Church because he sensed there the fakery of claiming allegiance to God yet living life internally by breaking them for selfish reasons. To young boy Jung this was a blasphemy of God, not a worship and submission. In these old age reflections on his life, which he insisted should only be published posthumously, Jung at last could admit publicly what a close relationship he has had with God all his life.

Jung's Search for the True God

Jung's relationship to God was close, intimate, total, and innocent. How else could he know, even as young boy, that his religion and acculturated faith has become falsified and wrongly justified, thus no longer a worship but a blasphemy? This can be seen in what he writes: "for I knew, knew from experience, that this grace was accorded only to one who fulfilled the will of God without reservation." He knew this as a young boy, having figured it out all by himself and being afraid to tell anyone of this big secret.

One can feel an attraction for this pathetic and deeply perceptive young person who is filled with "anxiety dreams" and night terrors of psychic, supernatural, and religious significance to him. And because Jung was sincere and innocent, God gave him an intimate relationship with Himself, opening the little boy's inner eyes to sense and perceive the real life that he later came to call the collective unconscious. He did not know it yet at this time that what he saw were spiritual representations expressed symbolically as natural looking apparitions in dreams, visions, and reflections. Later he became intensely interested in this symbolic language of the human psyche and came to describe it in terms of universal and biological archetypes. When these symbols are taken into the conscious mind through their spiritual meaning they deliver to the person the power from the unconscious.

Jung shares here his personal insight of himself as Personality 1 and Personality 2. One is the inherited and acculturated selfish and deceptive self. This used to put him into trouble with teachers and authority figures. Personality 2 was the real Jung who had but little interest in relating to the two-faced self-involved ordinary neighbors and citizens that made up the social life of Personality 1. The outer Jung was cold, calculating, and separated, while the inner Jung was passionate and in spiritual relationship with God and the people who inhabited the collective unconscious. This was the source of his cognitions about the invisible, subtle, second world: "*In my life No. 2 has been of prime importance, and I have always tried to make room for anything that wanted to come to me from within*". Jung later says in his autobiography:

Naturally I compensated my inner insecurity by an outward show of security, or--to put it better--the defect compensated itself without the intervention of my will. That is, I found myself being guilty and at the same time wishing to be innocent. Somewhere deep in the background I always knew that I was two persons.

One was the son of my parents, who went to school and was less intelligent, attentive, hard-working, decent, and clean than many other boys. The other was grown up--old, in fact--skeptical, mistrustful, remote from the world of men, but close to nature, the earth, the sun, the moon, the weather, a living creatures, and above all close to the night, to dreams, and to whatever "God" worked directly in him. I put "God" in quotation marks here. For nature seemed, like myself, to have been set aside by God as non-divine, although created by Him as an expression of Himself. Nothing could persuade me that "in the image of God" applied only to man.

In fact it seemed to me that the high mountains, the rivers, lakes, trees, flowers, and animals far better exemplified the essence of God than men with their ridiculous clothes, their meanness, vanity, mendacity, and abhorrent egotism-- all qualities with which I was only too familiar from myself, that is, from personality No. 1, the schoolboy of 1890. Besides his world there existed another realm, like a temple in which anyone who entered was transformed and suddenly overpowered by a vision of the whole cosmos, so that he could only marvel and admire, forgetful of himself. Here lived the "Other," who knew God as a hidden, personal, and at the same time suprapersonal secret. Here nothing separated man from God; indeed, it was as though the human mind looked down upon Creation simultaneously with God. (Jung, Memories, 63)

Swedenborg defines innocence as the essential trait needed for regeneration and salvation. The state of spiritual innocence is strong in infancy, then gradually weakens at around age seven when the individual begins be in business for self. Until that point there is a reliance on authority and order even though there is also a rebellion against it. Gradually the rebellion destroys the innocence and the individual begins to operate on principles that are called by Swedenborg *"for the sake of self only"*. This is the end of innocence and the end of reception of spiritual truths. Children receive spiritual truths without internal resistance.

When their innocence ends however, and they begin to look to self only, internal resistance to spiritual truths solidifies and bars entry into consciousness. In that devolved anti-human state of mind there is attraction felt for insincere faith that does not insist on the return to innocence and truth. Thus we can continue with our selfishness, deception, and cruelty without guilt and without the requirement to give it up as a sin against God and opposed to one's salvation. Jung passionately fought against this culturally inherited spiritual plague in himself by holding on to dear life within himself. This real life was the presence of God with us, and our relationship to God. Jung asserted this as a biological genetic and spiritually embedded necessity for our deepest and most sublime area of the self, called the soul.

> It would be blasphemy to assert that God can manifest Himself everywhere save only in the human soul. Indeed the very intimacy of the relationship between God and the soul automatically precludes any devaluation of the latter. It would be going perhaps too far to speak of an affinity; but at all events the soul must contain in itself the faculty of relation to God, i.e. a correspondence, otherwise a connection could never come about. This correspondence is, in psychological terms, the archetype of the God-image. (Jung, *Psychology and Alchemy*, CW 12, par. 11)

Jung early on as a teenager had already figured out the difference between good and evil. Ordinarily this does not happen until adult life. Until then it is normal to rely on received ideas and principles from parents, education, one's readings, and today, the media. Jung's innocence and acceptance of God's commandments as applying to him allowed the opening of his spiritual understanding so that he could recognize the falsity of the Church doctrine and faith that allow people to continue to break the commandments. Young precocious Jung saw that in this context, sermons in Church were a hoax and a blasphemy. He hated going back there and witnessing the charade.

Later as a young adult when he was in medical school Jung apparently read several of Swedenborg books according to his own statements. We can only wonder whether he found in them rational confirmation of what he had been given to see as a schoolboy. Here is an example where Swedenborg discusses the distinction between mere faith and faith that is from charity. The former is hypocritical faith of the lips only, the latter is genuine faith in charity, intention, and deed. Swedenborg's use of faith is in the sense of "*rational faith*" in contrast to "*blind faith*". The latter is the usual association among Christians. However Swedenborg defined faith as the acquisition from *Sacred Scripture* of spiritual-rational truths about God. He placed this in the understanding as a cognitive function. These truths are dead in themselves until they are vivified when the person acts according to these truths. This is called '*faith from charity*', namely, to will well to others and to be useful to society and community from a love of God.

> But the man who divides the Lord, charity, and faith, is not a form that receives but a form that destroys them. For he who separates the Lord from charity and faith, separates life from them, and when this is done, charity and faith either cease to exist or are abortions. That the Lord is life itself may be seen above (n. 358). He who acknowledges the Lord and sets charity aside, acknowledges Him with the lips only; his acknowledgment and confession is purely cold; within which there is no faith; for it lacks spiritual essence, since the essence of faith is charity. . (Swedenborg, True Christian Religion, n. 367)

Jung had precociously figured out early in his young life that religion is useless when it is merely believed but not practiced. He was able to see that "faith" is worthless unless it is joined to practicing the Commandments of life. Anyone could know this by reading many passages in the *New Testament* where it is declared that living well by not harming others is a necessary part to worshipping God. Swedenborg ties faith to "charity", which is defined as not harming others and not breaking the Commandments. For most Christians "charity" is taken to refer to benefiting the poor and giving money to charitable organizations. But in Swedenborg charity refers to the intention of wishing well and doing well to others for the sake of God.

> Faith separate from charity is not faith, because faith is the light of man's life and charity is its heat; therefore the separation of charity from faith is like the separation of heat from light; man's state then becomes like that of the world in winter, when everything on the earth dies. For charity to be charity and faith to be faith they can no more be separated than the will and the understanding; if these are separated the understanding comes to nothing, and presently the will also. It is the same with charity and faith, because charity resides in the will, and faith in the understanding.

> As there are these two, namely, good and truth, in each thing and in all things that have essential existence, so there are charity and faith, charity because it belongs to good, and faith because it belongs to truth. This may be illustrated by comparisons with many things in the human body, and with

many things on the earth. They maybe fitly compared with the respiration of the lungs and the systolic motion of the heart; since charity can no more be separated from faith than the heart from the lungs; for when the pulsation of the heart ceases, immediately the respiration of the lungs ceases; and when the respiration of the lungs ceases, all senses faint, all the muscles are deprived of motion, and in a short time the heart stops also and the life is wholly gone.

This is a proper comparison, because the heart corresponds to the will and thus to charity, and the respiration of the lungs to the understanding, and thus to faith; for (as said above) charity resides in the will, and faith in the understanding; and this is what "heart" and "breath" mean in the Word.

Charity conjoined with faith, and faith in its turn with charity, may be likened to the face of a handsome virgin beautiful from the intermingling of red and white. This again is a proper comparison, since love and charity therefrom in the spiritual world are red from the fire of the sun there, while truth and faith therefrom are white from the light of that sun; and therefore charity separate from faith may be likened to a face inflamed with pimples, and faith separate from charity to the pallid face of a corpse. Faith separate from charity may also be likened to a paralysis of one side, which is called hemiplegia, from which, when it increases, the man dies. It may also be compared to St. Vitus' dance, or to the dance of St. Guy, which is caused by the bite of the tarantula.

The rational faculty becomes like a man so bitten; like him it dances furiously and so deems itself alive, when yet it can no more collect various reasons into one, and think about spiritual truths, than one can when asleep in bed oppressed with a nightmare. This will suffice to demonstrate the two points of this chapter: first, That faith without charity is not faith, and that charity without faith is not charity, and that neither has life except from the Lord; secondly, That the Lord, charity, and faith make one, like life, will, and understanding in man; and if they are divided each perishes, like a pearl reduced to powder. (Swedenborg, True Christian Religion, n. 367)

At an early age Jung's precocious enlightenment did not need a formal doctrine such as expressed by Swedenborg in order for Jung to reflect rationally upon the spectacle of religious pretenses in his society. Later as a young man in medical school he may have come across the passage above from Swedenborg that discusses the difference between what is good and evil in the human mind based on the quality of one's love. Jung saw even at this early age that the critical issue for religion or faith has to do with the consequences. Religion is not real if it doesn't have consequences. Jung understood that heaven and hell are real and they are the consequences of religion. A false worship and doctrine does not require a conscience or a character rebirth. But true worship requires cessation of sinning. There is no eternal forgiveness through falsified faith. Later, Jung could have read in Swedenborg that we have loves from heaven and loves from hell in our mind. Jung felt the daily tug of war between 'the good Jung' (Personality 2) and 'the bad Jung' (Personality 1). His eternal happiness or torment was at stake. He knew it.

Jung's Unorthodox Vision of the Church

Jung describes this remarkable episode when he was about 12 or 13 years old (autobiography p. 52ff):

One fine summer day that same year I came out of school at noon and went to the cathedral square. The sky was gloriously blue, the bay one of radiant sunshine. The roof of the cathedral glittered, the sun sparkling from the new, brightly glazed tiles. I was overwhelmed by the beauty of the sight, and thought:

"The world is beautiful and the church is beautiful, and God made all this and sits above it far away in the blue sky on a golden throne and..."

Here came a great hole in my thoughts, and a choking sensation. I felt numbed, and knew only: "Don't go on thinking now! Something terrible is coming, something I do not want to think, something I dare not even approach. Why not? Because I would be committing the most frightful of sins. What is the most terrible sin? Murder? No, it can't be that. The most terrible sin is the sin against the Holy Ghost, which cannot be forgiven. Anyone who commits that sin is damned to hell for all eternity. That would be very sad for my parents, if their only son, to whom they are so attached, should be doomed to eternal damnation. I cannot do that to my parents. All I need do is not go on thinking."

That was easier said than done. On my long walk home I tried to think all sorts of other things, but I found my thoughts returning again and again to the beautiful cathedral which I loved so much, and to God sitting on the throne-- and then my thoughts would fly off again as if they had received a powerful electric shock. I kept repeating to myself: "Don't think of it, just don't think of it"

I reached home in a pretty worked-up state. My mother noticed that something was wrong, and asked, "What is the matter with you? Has something happened at school?" I was able to assure her, without lying, that nothing had happened at school. I did have the thought that it might help me if I could confess to my mother the real reason for my turmoil. But to do so I would have to do the very thing that seemed impossible: think my thought right to the end. The poor dear was utterly unsuspecting and could not possibly know that I was in terrible danger of committing the unforgivable sin and plunging myself into hell.

I rejected the idea of confessing and tried to efface myself as much as possible. That night I slept badly; again and again the forbidden thought, which I did not yet know, tried to break out, and I struggled desperately to fend it off. The next two days were sheer torture, and my mother was convinced that I was ill. But I resisted the temptation to confess, aided by the thought that it would cause my parents intense sorrow.

On the third night, however, the torment became so unbearable that I no longer knew what to do. I awoke from a restless sleep just in time to catch myself thinking again about the cathedral and God. I had almost continued the thought! I felt my resistance weakening. Sweating with fear, I sat up in bed to shake off sleep. "Now it is coming, now--it's serious! I must think. It must be thought out beforehand. Why should I think something I do not know? I don't want to, by God, that's sure. But who wants me to? Who wants to force me to think something I don't know and don't want to know? Where does this terrible will come from? And why should I be the one to be subjected to it?

I was thinking praises of the Creator of this beautiful world, I was grateful to him for this immeasurable gift, so why should I have to think something inconceivably wicked? I don't know what it is, I really don't, for I cannot and must not come anywhere near this thought, for that would be to risk thinking it at once. I haven't done this or wanted this, it has come on me like a bad dream. Where do such things come from? This has happened to me without my doing. Why? After all, I didn't create myself, I came into the world the way God made me--that is, the way I was shaped by my parents. Or can it have been that my parents wanted something of this sort? But my good parents would never have had any thoughts like that. Nothing so atrocious would ever have occurred to them."

I found this idea utterly absurd. Then I thought of my grandparents, whom I knew only from their portraits. They looked benevolent and dignified enough to repulse any idea that they might possibly be to blame. I mentally ran through the long procession of unknown ancestors until finally I arrived at Adam and Eve. And with them came the decisive thought: Adam and Eve were the first people; they had no parents, but were created directly by God, who intentionally made them as they were.

They had no choice but to be exactly the way God had created them. Therefore they did not know how they could possibly be different. They were perfect creatures of God, for He creates only perfection, and yet they committed the first sin by doing what God did not want them to do. How was that possible? They could not have done it if God had not placed in them the possibility of doing it. That was clear, too, from the serpent, whom God had created before them, obviously so that it could induce Adam and Eve to sin. God in His omniscience had arranged everything so that the first parents would have to sin.

Therefore it was God' s intention that they should sin. This thought liberated me instantly from my worst torment, since I now knew that God Himself had placed me in this situation. At first I did not know whether He intended me to commit my sin or not. I no longer thought of praying for illumination, since God had landed me in this fix without my willing it and had left me without any help. I was certain that I must search out His intention myself, and seek the way out alone.

At this point another argument began. "What does God want? To act or not to act? I must find out what God wants with me, and I must find out right away." I was aware, of course, that according to conventional morality there was no question but that sin must be avoided. That was what I had been doing up to now, but I knew I could not go on doing it. My broken sleep and my spiritual distress had worn me out to such a point that fending off the thought was tying me into unbearable knots. This could not go on. At the same time, I could not yield before I understood what God's will was and what He intended. For I was now certain that He was the author of this desperate problem.

Oddly enough, I did not think for a moment that the devil might be playing a trick on me. The devil played little part in my mental world at that time, and in any case regarded him as powerless compared with God. But from the moment I emerged from the mist and became conscious of myself, the unity, the greatness, and the superhuman majesty of God began to haunt my imagination. Hence there was no question in my mind but that God Himself was arranging a decisive test for me, and that everything depended on my understanding Him correctly. I knew, beyond a doubt, that I would ultimately be compelled to break down, to give way, but I did not want it to happen without my understanding it, since the salvation of my eternal soul was at stake.

God knows that I cannot resist much longer, and He does not help me, although I am on the point of having to commit the unforgivable sin. In His omnipotence He could easily lift this compulsion from me, but evidently He is not going to. Can it be that He wishes to test my obedience by imposing on me the unusual task of doing something against my own moral judgment and against the teachings of my religion, and even against His own commandment, something I am resisting with all my strength because I fear eternal damnation? Is it possible that God wishes to see whether I am capable of obeying His will even though my faith and my reason raise before me the specters of death and hell? That might really be the answer!

But these are merely my own thoughts. I may be mistaken. I dare not trust my own reasoning as far as that. I must think it all through once more." I thought it over again and arrived at the same conclusion.

Obviously God also desires me to show courage," I thought. "If that is so and I go through with it, then He will give me His grace and illumination? I gathered all my courage, as though I were about to leap forthwith into hell-fire, and let the thought come. I saw before me the cathedral, the blue sky. God sits on His golden throne, high above the world--and from under the throne an enormous turd falls upon the sparkling new roof, shatters it, and breaks the walls of the cathedral asunder. (p. 58)

So that was it! I felt an enormous, an indescribable relief. Instead of the expected damnation, grace had come upon me, and with it an unutterable bliss such as I had never known. I wept for happiness and gratitude. The wisdom and goodness of God had been revealed to me now that I had yielded 'to His inexorable command. It was as though I had experienced an illumination. A great many things I had not previously understood became clear to me. That was what my father had not understood, I thought he had failed to experience the will of God, had opposed it for the best reasons and out of the deepest faith. And that was why he had never

experienced the miracle of grace which heals all and makes all comprehensible. He had taken the Bible's commandments as his guide; he believed in God as the Bible prescribed and as his forefathers had taught him. But he did not know the immediate living God who stands, omnipotent and free, above His Bible and His

Church, who calls upon man to partake of His freedom, and can force him to renounce his own views and convictions in order to fulfill without reserve the command of God. In His trial of human courage God refuses to abide by traditions, no matter how sacred. In His omnipotence He will see to it that nothing really evil comes of such tests of courage. If one fulfills the will of God one can be sure of going the right way.

God had also created Adam and Eve in such a way that they had to think what they did not at all want to think. He had done that in order to find out whether they were obedient. And He could also demand something of me that I would have had to reject on traditional religious grounds. It was obedience which brought me grace, and after that experience I knew what God's grace was. One must be utterly abandoned to God; nothing matters but fulfilling His will. Otherwise all is folly and meaninglessness. From that moment on, when I experienced grace, my true responsibility began. Why did God befoul His cathedral? That, for me, was a terrible thought. But then came the dim understanding that God could be something terrible. I had experienced a dark and terrible secret. It overshadowed my whole life, and I became deeply pensive.

The experience also had the effect of increasing my sense of inferiority. I am a devil or a swine, I thought; I am infinitely depraved. But then I began searching through the New Testament and read, with a certain satisfaction, about the Pharisee and the publican, and that reprobates are the chosen ones. It made a lasting impression on me that the unjust steward was praised, and that Peter, the waverer, was appointed the rock upon which the Church was built. The greater my inferiority feelings became, the more incomprehensible did God's grace appear to me. After all, I had never been sure of myself. When my mother once said to me, "You have always been a good boy, I simply could not grasp it. I a good boy? That was quite new to me. I often thought of myself as a corrupt and inferior person. With the experience of God and the cathedral I at last had something tangible that was part of the great secret--as if I had always talked of stones falling from heaven and now had one in my pocket. But actually, it was a shaming experience. I had fallen into something bad, something evil and sinister, though at the same time it was a kind of distinction. Sometimes I had an overwhelming urge to speak, not about that, but only to hint that there were some curious things about me which no one knew of. I wanted to find out whether other people had undergone similar experiences. I never succeeded in discovering so much as a trace of them in others. As a result, I had the feeling that I was either outlawed or elect, accursed or blessed.

This sense of election led to a final disillusionment with the Church on the occasion of his First Communion. He had been led to believe that this would be a great experience. Instead, nothing. He concluded: "For me, it was an absence of God and no religion. Church was a place to which I no longer could go. There was no life there, but death." (Jung, Memories, p.73)

Jung was able to experience the spiritual presence of God with himself. His faith was alive because he made charity an essential part of it. He did this from innocence and inner prompting that he honored. At that early time in his life Jung could not have known with doctrinal clarity why the faith of his parents and co-religionists was dead and worthless for their salvation and eternal life. He thought that it was because they did not wish or seek to experience the presence of God phenomenologically in their lives. They thus did not have a living personal relationship with God. Their faith did not prevail for them because they did not know God. And they did not know God because they were unwilling to stop being selfish and self-centered.

Here is Jung's statement in 1944, as he was ending his seventh decade of life, on why he is not a "professed" Catholic though he is a "practical Christian":

WHY I AM NOT A CATHOLIC!

Firstly: Because I am a practical Christian to whom love and justice to his brother mean more than dogmatic speculations about whose ultimate truth or untruth no human being can ever have certain knowledge.

The relation to my brother and the unity of the true "catholic" Christendom is to me infinitely more important than "justification by fide sola." As a Christian I have to share the burden of my brother's wrongness, and that is most heavy when I do not know whether in the end he is not more right than I. I hold it to be immoral, in any case entirely unchristian, to put my brother in the wrong (i.e., to call him fool, ass, spiteful, obdurate, etc.) simply because I suppose myself to be in possession of the absolute truth. Every totalitarian claim gradually isolates itself because it excludes so many people as "defectors, lost, fallen, apostate, heretic," and so forth. The totalitarian maneuvers himself into a corner, no matter how large his original following.

I hold all confessionalism to be completely unchristian.

Secondly: Because I am a doctor. If I possessed the absolute truth I could do nothing further than to press into my patient's hand a book of devotion or confessional guidance, just what is no longer of any help to him. When, on the other hand, I discover in his untruth a truth, in his confusion an order, in his lostness something that has been found, then I have helped him. This requires an incomparably greater self-abnegation and self-surrender for my brother's sake than if I assessed, correctly from the standpoint of one confession, the motivations of another.

You underestimate the immense number of those of goodwill, but to whom confessionalism blocks the doors. A Christian has to concern himself, especially if he is a physician of souls, with the spirituality of the reputedly unspiritual (spirit = confessionalism!) and he can do this only if he speaks their language and certainly not if, in the deterrent way of confessionalism, he sounds the kerygmatik trumpet, hoarse with age. Whoever talks in today's world of an absolute and single truth is speaking in an obsolete dialect and not in any way in the language of mankind. Christianity possesses a day of love, good tidings from God, but no textbook of a dogma with claim to totality.

Therefore it is hard to understand why God should never have sent more than one message. Christian modesty in any case strictly forbids assuming that God did not send εαγγλια in other languages, not just in Greek, to other nations. If we think otherwise our thinking is in the deepest sense unchristian. The Christian-my idea of Christian-knows no curse formulas; indeed he does not even sanction the curse put on the innocent fig-tree by the rabbi Jesus, nor does he lend his ear to the missionary Paul of Tarsus when he forbids cursing to the Christian and then he himself curses the next moment.

Thirdly: Because I am a man of science. The Catholic doctrine, as you present it to me so splendidly, is familiar to me to that extent. I am convinced of its "truth" in so far as it formulates determinable psychological facts, and thus far I accept this truth without further ado. But where I lack such empirical psychological foundations it does not help me in the least to believe in anything beyond them, for that would not compensate for my missing knowledge; nor could I ever surrender to the self-delusion of knowing something where I merely believe. I am now nearly seventy years old, but the charisma of belief has never arisen in me. Perhaps I am too overweening, too conceited; perhaps you are right in thinking that the cosmos circles around the God Jung. But in any case I have never succeeded in thinking that what I believe, feel, think, and understand is the only and final truth and that I enjoy the unspeakable privilege of God-likeness by being the possessor of the sole truth. You see that, although I can estimate the charisma of faith and its blessedness, the acceptance of "faith" is impossible for me because it says nothing to me.

You will naturally remonstrate that, after all, I talk about "God." I do this with the same right as humanity has from the beginning equated the numinous effects of certain psychological facts with an unknown primal cause called God. This cause is beyond my understanding, and therefore I can say nothing further about it except that I am convinced of the existence of such a cause, and indeed with the same logic by which one may conclude from the disturbance of a planet's course the existence of a yet unknown heavenly body. To be sure, I do not believe in the absolute validity of the law of causality, which is why I guard against "positing" God as cause, for by this I would have given him a precise definition.

Such restraint is surely an offense to confessors of the Faith.

But according to the fundamental Christian commandment I must not only bear with and understand my schismatic Protestant brother, but also my brothers in Arabia and India. They, too, have received strange but no less notable tidings which it is my obligation to understand. As a European, I am burdened most heavily by my unexpectedly dark brother, who confronts me with his antichristian Neo-Paganism. This extends far beyond the borders of Germany as the most pernicious schism that has ever beset Christianity. And though I deny it a thousand times, it is also in me. One cannot come to terms with this conflict by imputing wrong to someone else and the undoubted right to oneself.

This conflict I can solve first of all only within myself and not in another. [CW 18:1466-1472]

To understand Jung's position on religion and God it helps to consider the essential distinction Jung maintains between religious dogma and personal experience of a relationship with God. He rejects "confessionalism" which is the idea that salvation comes from a faith that is based on some specific belief rather than on understanding: "I hold all confessionalism to be completely unchristian" Jung rejects the silencing of rational thinking that comes with "blind faith". It is called "blind" as a result of avoiding rational understanding: *"the acceptance of "faith" is impossible for me because it says nothing to me"* and *"nor could I ever surrender to the self-delusion of knowing something where I merely believe"*.

The same essential distinction is made by Swedenborg:

THE NATURE OF FAITH THAT IS SEPARATED FROM CHARITY. In order that it may be seen what the character of faith is when separated from charity, I will present it in its nakedness, in which it is as follows: God the Father, being angry with mankind, cast them away from Him, and out of justice resolved to take vengeance by their eternal condemnation and He said to the Son, "Go down, fulfill the law, and take upon Thyself the condemnation destined for them, and then perchance I shall be moved to compassion." Wherefore He came down, and fulfilled the law; and suffered Himself to be hanged on the cross, and cruelly put to death. When this was done, He returned to the Father and said, "I have taken upon Myself the condemnation of mankind, therefore now be merciful;" thus interceding for them But He received for answer, "Toward them I cannot; but as I saw Thee upon the cross, and beheld then Thy blood, I have been moved to compassion. Nevertheless I will not pardon them, but I will impute unto them Thy merit, but to none others than those who acknowledge this. This shall be the faith by which they can be saved."

Such is that faith in its nakedness. Who that possesses any enlightened reason does not see in it absurdities that are contrary to the Divine essence itself? As for instance that God, who is love itself, and mercy itself, could out of anger and its consequent revengefulness condemn men and accurse them to hell. Or again, that He wills to be moved to mercy by His Son's taking upon

Him their condemnation, and by the sight of His suffering upon the cross, and of His blood. Who that possesses any enlightened reason does not see that the Deity could not say to another coequal Deity, "I do not pardon them, but I impute to them Thy merit?" Or, "Now let them live as they please; only let them believe this and they shall be saved." Besides many other absurdities.

The reason why these absurdities have not been seen is that they have induced a blind faith, and have thereby shut men's eyes, and stopped up their ears. Shut men's eyes and stop up their ears, that is, contrive that they do not exercise thought from any understanding, and then say whatever you please to persons on whom some idea of eternal life has been imprinted, and they will believe it; even if you should say that God is capable of being angry and of breathing vengeance; that God is capable of inflicting eternal condemnation on any one; that God wills to be moved to mercy through the blood of His Son; that He will impute and attribute this to man as merit and as man's; and that He will save him by his merely thinking so. Or again, that one God could bargain such things with another God of the one essence, and impose them upon Him; and other things of the same kind. But open your eyes and unstop your ears, that is, think about these things from understanding, and you will see their incongruity with the real truth. [Swedenborg, Doctrine of Faith, 44-46]

Jung is able to reject these dogmatic prescriptions on the scientific ground that these dogmatic notions are not psychologically real: *"You see that, although I can estimate the charisma of faith and its blessedness, the acceptance of "faith" is impossible for me because it says nothing to me."* Swedenborg puts the same point this way, referring to our angelic state of consciousness:

This then is the reason why those who are in the spiritual affection of truth possess an internal acknowledgment of truth. As the angels are in this affection, they discard the dogma that the understanding must be kept in obedience to faith, and say, "What is this? believing when you do not see whether the thing is true?" And if somebody says that still it is to be believed, they reply, "Do you consider yourself the Deity that I am bound to believe you? or do you think me mad enough to believe a statement in which I do not see the truth? Cause me to see it." Thereupon the dogmatizer betakes himself elsewhere. The wisdom of the angels consists solely in this: that they see and comprehend everything they think about. [Swedenborg, Doctrine of Faith, 4]

Swedenborg's reference to an "*internal acknowledgment of truth*" is the very method Jung used for himself when refusing to believe the dogmas of his family inherited religion because they had no personal meaning or reality for him. Jung writes: "*I am a practical Christian to whom love and justice to his brother mean more than dogmatic speculations*". Jung's rejection of religious dogma opened up his mind to the reality of a relationship with God. The psychological experience of this reality allowed Jung to comprehend that God is universal in the sense that He maintains a relationship with every culture and its religion. For one religion to then condemn another is fruitless and immoral, thus not just and spiritual. Jung says: "Therefore it is hard to understand why God should never have sent more than one message".

Swedenborg also affirms the universality of God and puts it this way:

> *Belief in God and refusal to do evil because it is against God are the two elements that make a religion a religion. If either is lacking, we cannot call it a religion, since believing in God and doing evil are mutually contradictory, as are doing what is good and not believing in God. Neither is possible apart from the other.*

> *The Lord has provided that there should be some religion almost everywhere and that everyone who believes in God and does not do evil because it is against God should have a place in heaven. Heaven, seen in its entirety, looks like a single individual, whose life or soul is the Lord. In that heavenly person there are all the components that there are in a physical person, differing the way heavenly things differ from earthly ones.*

> *We know that there are within us not only the parts formed as organs from blood vessels and nerve fibers--the forms we call our viscera. There are also skin, membranes, tendons, cartilage, bones, nails, and teeth. They are less intensely alive than the organic forms, which they serve as ligaments, coverings, and supports. If there are to be all these elements in that heavenly person who is heaven, it cannot be made up of the people of one religion only. It needs people from many religions; so all the people who make these two universal principles of the church central to their own lives have a place in that heavenly person, that is, in heaven. They enjoy the happiness that suits their own nature. [Swedenborg, Divine Providence 326]*

Both Jung and Swedenborg affirm the spiritual principle that any individual can enjoy eternal heavenly consciousness and happiness who possesses a character that inwardly feels goodwill towards others. Jung put it this way:

"But according to the fundamental Christian commandment I must not only bear with and understand my schismatic Protestant brother, but also my brothers in Arabia and India. They, too, have received strange but no less notable tidings which it is my obligation to understand."

All religions acknowledge God's existence and a life after death in accordance with how one has lived in this life. Such as one has become in this life, such will one be in the afterlife. The two phases of the ego – pre-death and post-death – are connected by cause-effect karma. Jung was shocked by witnessing the people of his childhood religion and culture break all the commandments that they recited with insincere piety. They felt no moral or spiritual obligation, thus no Christian charity, to those who did not profess to their specific dogmas. They believed that everyone in this church were saved and everyone else in the universe were condemned. This is the "faith alone" Christianity that despises the works of charity despite many statements by Jesus in the New Testament specifying that faith is what love does to others, thus charity. Faith without that charity is no saving faith. To those who have this faith Jesus says "depart from Me all ye workers of iniquity", as brought up by Swedenborg:

That such a lot awaits those who are in faith alone and in no charity, was foretold by the Lord in many passages. Thus in Matthew:
Every tree that bringeth not forth good fruit is hewn down, and cast into the fire; therefore by their fruits ye shall know them. Not everyone that saith unto Me, Lord, Lord, shall enter into the kingdom of the heavens, but he that doeth the will of My Father who is in the heavens. Many shall say to Me in that day, Lord, Lord, have we not prophesied by Thy name, and by Thy name cast out demons, and in Thy name done many powers? And then will I confess unto them, I never knew you; depart from Me all ye workers of iniquity. Every one that heareth My words and doeth them, I will liken to a prudent man, who built his house upon a rock. And everyone that heareth My words and doeth them not, shall be likened to a foolish man who built his house upon the sand (Matt. 7:19-27).

Here those who are in faith from charity, and those who are in faith and in no charity are described; those who are in faith from charity, by "the tree bearing good fruit," and by "the house that was built upon a rock;" "fruits" moreover signify in the Word the works of charity and a "rock" faith from charity; but those who are in faith separate from charity are meant by "the tree that bringeth forth no good fruit," and by those "building a house upon the sand," "evil fruit" moreover signifies in the Word evil works, and "sand" faith separate from charity. Of such it is said that they will say, "Lord, Lord, open to us," but that the reply will be, "I never knew you; depart from Me, all ye workers of iniquity." [Swedenborg, Apocalypse Explained 212]

Jung saw the iniquity of the religious and he came to see religion as an impediment to the experiencing of God through self-denial and consequent obedience to God's will. Here is a selection of statements Jung has made about **religion**:

a) *"Religion is a defense against the experience of God"* [Quoted by Joseph Campbell]

b) *"Religions are a substitute for legitimate suffering"* [unknown]

c) *What is ordinarily called "religion" is a substitute. ... The substitute has the obvious purpose of replacing immediate [religious] experience by a choice of suitable symbols supported by an organized dogma and ritual."* (from "Psychology and Religion", 1938)

d) *All religions are therapies for the sorrows and disorders of the soul."* (from "Commentary to The Secret of the Golden Flower", 1929)

e) *"I have treated many hundreds of patients. Among those in the second half of life - that is to say, over 35 - there has not been one whose problem in the last resort was not that of finding a religious outlook on life. It is safe to say that every one of them fell ill because he had lost that which the living religions of every age have given their followers, and none of them has really been healed who did not regain his religious outlook."* — C.G. Jung (Modern Man in Search of a Soul)

f) *"No matter what the world thinks about religious experience, the one who has it possesses a great treasure, a thing that has become for him a source of life, meaning, and beauty, and that has given a new splendor to the world and to mankind. ... Where is the criterion by which you could say that such a life is not legitimate, that such an experience is not valid?"* (from "Psychology and Religion", 1938)

g) *Religious experience is absolute; it cannot be disputed. You can only say that you have never had such an experience, whereupon your opponent will reply: "Sorry, I have." And there the discussion will end." (from "Psychology and Religion", 1938)*

Reference Notes to Chapter 2

(1) Tympas, G. C. (2014). *Carl Jung and Maximus the Confessor: On Psychic Development*. London: Routledge, p. 48-49

(2) Swedenborg, E. (1745). *Arcana Coelestia* (Heavenly Secrets).

(3) James, Leon. (2015). A comparison of keywords in the dynamic psychology of Jung, Swedenborg, and Freud. *Journal of Psychology and Clinical Psychiatry*, Vol. 3 (3), 00134, 1-13.)

(4) Taylor, Eugene. (2006). Jung and His Intellectual context: the Swedenborgian Connection. *Studia Swedenborgiana*,1974-2006. Accessible document at: http://www.shs.psr.edu/studia/index.asp?article_id=77

(5) James, H. (1884). The literary remains of the late Henry James. Houghton Mifflin.

(6) James, W. (1985). *The varieties of religious experience* (Vol. 13). Harvard University Press.
James, W. (2004). *The Principles of Psychology* (Volume 1 of 2). Digireads. com Publishing.

The Chinese philosophy of yoga is based upon the fact of this instinctive preparation for death as a goal, and, following the analogy with the goal of the first half of life, namely, begetting and reproduction, the means towards perpetuation of physical life, it takes as the purpose of spiritual existence the symbolic begetting and bringing to birth of a psychic spirit body ('subtle body'), which ensures the continuity of the detached consciousness. ~Carl Jung, The Secret of the Golden Flower, Page 124.

Chapter 3
Jung and Swedenborg on Life After Death

Oh outstanding vessel of devotion and obedience! To the ancestral spirits of my most beloved and faithful wife Emma Maria. She completed her life and after her death she was lamented. She went over to the secret of eternity in the year 1955. Her age was 73. Her husband C.G. .Jung has made and placed [this stone] in 1956.

Jung's Analytical Psychology

A well known translator and editor of Jung's works opined as follows about him:

> *C. G. Jung is widely recognized as a major figure in modern Western thought, and his work continues to spark controversies. He played critical roles in the formation of modern psychology, psychotherapy, and psychiatry, and a large international profession of analytical psychologists world under his name. His world has had its widest impact, however, outside professional circles: Jung and Freud are the names that most people first think of in connection with psychology, and their ideas have been widely disseminated in the arts, the humanities, films, and popular culture. Jung is also widely regarded as one of the instigators of the New Age movement.* (Shamdasani, in Introduction to *Liber Novus*)

Jung's contribution to psychology went beyond Freud's contribution because Jung searched for the implications of the unconscious in more detail and in greater depth of dualism than Freud who was more intent on its significance for therapy and its relation to the physical body. Jung wrote about Freud:

> *Above all, psychoanalysis in the strictly Freudian sense is not only a therapeutic method but a psycho logical theory, which does not confine itself in the least to the neuroses and to psychopathology in general but attempts also to bring within its province the normal phenomenon of the dream and, besides this, wide areas of the humane sciences, of literature and the creative arts, as well as biography, mythology, folklore, comparative religion, and philosophy.* (Jung, in *Freud and Psychoanalysis*)
>
> ...
>
> *In order to interpret the products of the unconscious, I also found it necessary to give a quite different reading to dreams and fantasies. I did not reduce them to personal factors, as Freud does, but and this seemed indicated by their very nature I compared them with the symbols from mythology and the history of religion, in order to discover the meaning they were trying to express. This method did in fact yield extremely interesting results, not least because it permitted an entirely new reading of dreams and fantasies, thus making it possible to unite the otherwise incompatible and archaic tendencies of the unconscious with the conscious personality.*

This union had long seemed to me the end to strive for, because neurotics (and many normal people, too) suffer at bottom from a dissociation between conscious and unconscious. As the unconscious contains not only the sources of instinct and the whole prehistoric nature of man right down to the animal level, but also, along with these, the creative seeds of the future and the roots of all constructive fantasies, a separation from the unconscious through neurotic dissociation means nothing less than a separation from the source of all life.

It therefore seemed to me that the prime task of the therapist was to re-establish this lost connection and the life-giving co-operation between conscious and unconscious. Freud depreciates the unconscious and seeks safety in the discriminating power of consciousness. This approach is generally mistaken and leads to desiccation and rigidity wherever a firmly established consciousness already exists; for, by holding off the antagonistic and apparently hostile elements in the unconscious, it denies itself the vitality it needs for its own renewal. (Jung, in Freud and Psychoanalysis, 762)

This statement marks a decisive difference in outlook between Freud and Jung and brings him closer to the central focus on correspondences in Swedenborg's work.

According to Swedenborg's anatomical definition of consciousness the human mind operates at three different levels of perfection and complexity. These levels are arranged sequentially or progressively starting with the influx of Divine truth-substance, which forms the medium or substance of all consciousness. The Divine truth-substance (also called spiritual light) enters at the celestial level of the mind and produces the operations of celestial consciousness, which is the highest possible for finite human beings. From there truth-substance continues its descent into the spiritual consciousness level, and then the natural consciousness level, of which we are clearly aware in our daily life. The levels of operation in the mind that go on above the natural level are unconscious but vitally important. An acknowledgment of God in this top down operation is essential to keep the process flowing. A denial of God closes the flow. The individual is then trapped mentally in materialism, unable because unwilling, to understand the reality of the two worlds and of human immortality.

The normal and healthy functioning of our daily natural consciousness is dependent for its operation on the inflow of celestial and spiritual consciousness into the natural mind. This inflow is unconscious but its consequences are experienced as the ability for rational thinking and understanding. But when the spiritual operation is blocked from entry, the natural mind then deteriorates and experiences the symptoms of dysfunction and social conflict. The individual blocks the inflow of the unconscious spiritual thinking by denying the existence of God and life after death. When these are denied, the natural consciousness sinks to the bottom and becomes corporeal or sensual, unable to receive and be enriched by spiritual ideas given that these are denied. As Jung observes in the above quote, when the connection between the unconscious (or spiritual) and the conscious (or natural) is disrupted or cut off, the ego *"denies itself the vitality it needs for its own renewal"*. As a result, mental development is interrupted or deviated and wholeness is not achieved. This gives rise to abnormality and pathology in the personality structure.

More than Freud, Jung has had a specialized influence on the thinking and feeling of the current generation, which is the generation that follows Jung's passing on in 1961. We can review and appreciate that influence as it shows for instance, in a highly popular online encyclopedia produced and maintained by thousands of volunteers in many nations. From *Wikipedia* here are selections from the extensive entry on *Analytical Psychology*. It gives us an opportunity to observe how Jung's ideas have crossed into the psychic arena of popular consciousness. I have **bolded key words** to allow you to locate specific topics. I will comment and enlarge upon portions of the quote.

> ... *"As Jung said, "The beauty about the unconscious is that it is really unconscious". Hence, the unconscious is 'untouchable' by experimental researches, or indeed any possible kind of scientific or philosophical reach, precisely because it is unconscious. (...)*

> ... *The overarching goal of Jungian psychology is the attainment of Self through individuation.* **Jung defines "Self"** *as the "archetype of wholeness and the regulating center of the psyche." Central to this process is the individual's encounter with his/her psyche and the bringing of its elements into consciousness. Humans experience the unconscious through symbols encountered in all aspects of life: in dreams, art, religion, and the symbolic dramas we enact in our relationships and life pursuits. Essential to this numinous encounter is the merging of the individual's consciousness with the collective consciousness (sic) through this symbolic language. By means of*

bringing conscious awareness to that which is not conscious, unconscious elements can be integrated with consciousness when they "surface."

Note here several important ideas that we'll encounter later in our discussion. The "Self" (a word that Jung sometimes capitalized) is an archetype, specifically of wholeness in the personality. There are different elements of the Self-archetype that reside in the collective unconscious. These parts need to be brought into consciousness, and this is accomplished through symbols "encountered in all aspects of life". The symbolic language allows the "merging" of individual consciousness and collective unconscious. In this way conscious awareness is brought to that which is unconscious.

... *"**Neurosis**" results from a disharmony between the individual's (un)consciousness and his higher Self. The psyche is a self-regulating adaptive system. Humans are energetic systems, and if the energy gets blocked, the psyche gets stuck, or sick. If adaption is thwarted, the psychic energy will stop flowing, and regress. This process manifests in neurosis and psychosis. Human psychic contents are complex, and deep. They can schism, and split, and form **complexes that take over one's personality**. Jung proposed that this occurs through maladaptation to one's external or internal realities. The principles of adaptation, projection, and compensation are central processes in Jung's view of psyche's ability to adapt.*

... *The aim of **psychotherapy** is to assist the individual in reestablishing a healthy relationship to the unconscious: neither flooded by it (characteristic of psychosis, such as schizophrenia) or out of balance in relationship to it (as with neurosis, a state that results in depression, anxiety, and personality disorders).*

... *In order to undergo the **individuation process**, the individual must be open to the parts of oneself beyond one's own ego. The modern individual grows continually in psychic awareness (attention to dreams), explores the world of religion and spirituality, and questions the assumptions of the operant societal worldview rather than just blindly living life in accordance with dominant norms and assumptions.*

Jung contrasts the "ego" with the "Self". By integrating the unconscious elements of the Self one expands the ego and one is able to grow in psychic awareness. This is the process of individuation by which the ego gets to know and adapt to itself the unconscious parts of the Self. Psychotherapy assists the limited conscious ego in this task of larger integration with the unconscious. The healing integration process is helped by paying attention to dreams and exploring religious or spiritual ideas from an independent perspective. Dreams and symbols are methods by which the complex elements of the unconscious Self make themselves known to the ego consciousness.

> An innate need for self-realization leads people to explore and integrate these disowned parts of themselves. This natural process is called individuation, or the process of becoming an individual. ... According to Jung, **self-realization** is attained through **individuation**.

> Reliable communication between the conscious and unconscious parts of the psyche is necessary for **wholeness**.

> ... Also crucial is the belief that **dreams** show ideas, beliefs, and feelings of which individuals are not readily aware, but need to be, and that such material is expressed in a personalized vocabulary of visual metaphors. Things "known but unknown" are contained in the unconscious, and dreams are one of the main vehicles for the unconscious to express them.

> **Analytical psychology** distinguishes between a personal unconscious and a collective unconscious. The collective unconscious contains archetypes common to all human beings. That is, individuation may bring to surface symbols that do not relate to the life experiences of a single person. This content is more easily viewed as answers to the more fundamental questions of humanity: life, death, meaning, happiness, fear. Among these more spiritual concepts may arise and be integrated into the personality.

> **Archetypes are innate**, universal prototypes for ideas and may be used to interpret observations. A group of memories and interpretations associated with an archetype is a complex, e.g. a mother complex associated with the mother archetype.

> **Archetypes can grow on their own** and present themselves in a variety of creative ways. Jung began to see and talk to a manifestation of anima and that she taught him how to interpret dreams. As soon as he could interpret on his own, she ceased talking to him because she was no longer needed.

There is only one collective unconscious for the entire human race since its beginning, covering our past, present, and future. The content of the collective unconscious can be discussed in terms of archetypes. An individual archetype is a universal prototype that is applicable to every person and is innate with everyone as part of their humanity. Archetypes are spiritual meanings that are represented by images, symbols, and patterns. These spiritual meanings are actually anatomical objects or organs that are connected to our body organs. The appearance of an archetype in the conscious ego can assume a human form with which the person can dialog and discover new knowledge. This is one way that Jung learned how to interpret dreams.

Continuing with selected parts of the *Wikipedia* presentation on Jung:

> *In the second half of our lives*, *humans reunite with the human race. They become part of the collective once again. This is when adults start to contribute to humanity (volunteer time, build, garden, create art, etc.) rather than destroy. They are also more likely to pay attention to their unconscious and conscious feelings. Young men rarely say "I feel angry." or "I feel sad." This is because they have not yet rejoined the human collective experience, commonly reestablished in their older, wiser years. A common theme is for young rebels to "search" for their true selves and realize that a contribution to humanity is essentially a necessity for a whole self.*

> *Jung proposes that the ultimate goal of the collective unconscious and self-realization is* **to pull us to the highest experience***. This, of course,* **is spiritual***.*

> *If a* **person does not proceed toward self-knowledge***, neurotic symptoms may arise.* **Symptoms** *are widely defined, including, for instance, phobias, psychosis, and depression.*

The central feature of Jung's psychotherapy is the same feature that also applies to normal human development. This is the process of becoming an individual or person. This challenge begins when we reach young adulthood and social independence. For the person to avoid psychological dysfunctions contact must be made with the elements of self that are still located in the collective unconscious of humankind. Similarly, if the person has already fallen into various dysfunctions such as neuroses and psychoses, the way out of the impasse is to face the particular archetypes that compel us to live with the dysfunctions. The missing pieces that we need to individuate, that is, to become whole, must be found and acquired as one's own. This is necessary because they are our own. They may be positive or negative forces of personality, but if they are our own we must claim them.

Facing the dark forces of the collective unconscious and claiming the missing elements as our own, does not mean that we succumb to them passively. To do this would be deadly since the negative elements of our total Self are inherently evil and destructive. Facing them and owning them means to acknowledge their presence in us, locate them, identify them, and sequester them!

Once reintegrated as our own we have the power and privilege to dispose of them as we please. Not until then, for until then they are our feared enemy. They have this power from the outside, prior to their reintegration into our personhood. Once integrated, they are in our power system and disposition. Prior to integration or individuation the "shadow" content of the collective unconscious is repressed, denied, avoided, transmuted. There is no encountering. No opportunity for reversing and healing. Instead, the symptoms of neuroses and psychoses become substitute acknowledgments. These substitutes hide the origin or cause of the symptoms. It is a psychic dead-end process with no exit.

> The **shadow** is an unconscious complex defined as the repressed, suppressed or disowned qualities of the conscious self. The human being deals with the reality of the shadow in four ways: denial, projection, integration and/or transmutation. In its more constructive aspects, a person's shadow may represent hidden positive qualities. This has been referred to as the "gold in the shadow". Jung emphasized the importance of being aware of shadow material and incorporating it into conscious awareness in order to avoid projecting shadow qualities on others.

> Jung identified the **anima** as being the unconscious feminine component of men and the **animus** as the unconscious masculine component in women. Jung stated that the anima and animus act as guides to the unconscious unified Self, and that forming an awareness and a connection with the anima or animus is one of the most difficult and rewarding steps in psychological growth. Jung reported that he identified his anima as she spoke to him, as an inner voice, unexpectedly one day.

Jung attributes human **rational thought to be the male nature**, while the **irrational aspect is considered to be natural female** (rational being defined as involving judgment, irrational being defined as involving perceptions). Consequently, irrational moods are the progenies of the male anima shadow and irrational opinions of the female animus shadow. **[Note: Instead of "irrational" read "affective". For "rational" read "cognitive".]**

(Psycho)Analysis is a way to experience and integrate the unknown material. It is a search for the meaning of behaviours, symptoms and events. Many are the channels to reach this greater self-knowledge. The analysis of dreams is the most common. Others may include expressing feelings in art pieces, poetry or other expressions of creativity.

... According to Jung, the psyche is an apparatus for adaptation and orientation, and consists of a number of different **psychic functions**. Among these he distinguishes four basic functions:

sensation - perception by means of the sense organs [read: **affective and sensorimotor**];
intuition - perceiving in unconscious way or perception of unconscious contents. [read: **spiritual-rational and cognitive**]
thinking - function of intellectual cognition; the forming of logical conclusions; [read: **cognitive**]
feeling - function of subjective estimation; [read: **affective**]

... It is important to state that Jung seemed to often see his work as **not a complete psychology** in itself but as his unique contribution to the field of psychology. Jung claimed late in his career that only for about a third of his patients did he use "Jungian analysis." For another third, Freudian psychology seemed to best suit the patient's needs and for the final third Adlerian analysis was most appropriate. In fact, it seems that most contemporary Jungian clinicians merge a developmentally grounded theory, such as Self psychology or Donald Winnicott's work, with the Jungian theories in order to have a "whole" theoretical repertoire to do actual clinical work.

The **"I" or Ego** is tremendously important to Jung's clinical work. Jung's theory of etiology of psychopathology could almost be simplified to be stated as a **too rigid conscious attitude towards the whole of the psyche**. That is, a psychotic episode can be seen from a Jungian perspective as the "rest" of the *psyche overwhelming the conscious psyche because* **the conscious psyche effectively was locking out and repressing the psyche as a whole**.

(Wikipedia accessed January 2015 at
http://en.m.wikipedia.org/wiki/Analytical_psychology

Jung's Dualism

Jung's focus on the "symbols from mythology and the history of religion" is seen further developed by Swedenborg from the phenomenological perspective rather than literary. Swedenborg's dual consciousness brought him into direct conversational contact with people of the past who had lived on earth in ancient times.

> *Religion has existed from the most ancient times, and the inhabitants of the earth everywhere have had a knowledge of God, and some knowledge of a life after death. This has not originated from themselves or their own intelligence, but from the ancient Word, mentioned above; and in later times from the Israelitish Word. From these two Words forms of religion spread to the Indies and their islands; through Egypt and Ethiopia to the kingdoms of Africa, from the maritime parts of Asia to Greece, and thence to Italy. However, as the Word could only be written by representatives, that is, by such things in the world as correspond to, and consequently signify, heavenly things, religion with the Gentiles was turned into idolatry, and in Greece into mythology. Divine properties and attributes were turned into so many gods, and over these men set one supreme deity whom they called Jove, possibly from Jehovah; while it is well known that they had some conception of Paradise, some knowledge of the Flood, the sacred fire, and the four ages from the first or golden age to the last or iron age, as described in Daniel ii. 31-35.* (Swedenborg, *True Christian Religion* n. 275)

Jung did not possess Swedenborg's dual consciousness (and no one else did!) yet he was able to abstractly fathom the power and ubiquity of the psyche's world, a world Swedenborg called "the spiritual world of eternity" which overlapped with the mental world, thus setting an equality between mind and spirit.

Here is how Jung described his awe of the world of psyche that he knew to be non-spatial:

> I can only gaze with wonder and awe at the depths and heights of our psychic nature. Its non-spatial universe conceals an untold abundance of images which have accumulated over millions of years of living development and become fixed in the organism. My consciousness is like an eye that penetrates to the most distant spaces, yet it is the psychic non-ego that fills them with non-spatial images. And these images are not pale shadows, but tremendously powerful psychic factors. The most we may be able to do is misunderstand them, but we can never rob them of their power by denying them. Beside this picture I would like to place the spectacle of the starry heavens at night, for the only equivalent of the universe within is the universe without; and just as I reach this world through the medium of the body, so I reach that world through the medium of the psyche. (Jung, Freud and Psychoanalysis, 765).

Here Jung clearly perceives that our individual psyche or mind possesses an anatomical body by which to move around and be aware of the world of psyche, just as we have a physical body that we use to act in the physical world. It doesn't seem that Freud ever imagined the psyche or the unconscious to consist of an anatomy other than the physical body, and especially its brain. For Freud the mental was located in the physical. He did not apparently see that out of the physical the psychical cannot come or originate from. Freud's position was identical to the current position in neuroanatomy and neuroscience (e.g., Damasio). It is to Jung's credit that he did not fall for this centuries-old error. Swedenborg confirmed by daily observation over 27 years that our mind is a spiritual body and is active in the mental world of the afterlife of eternity.

Jung was therefore fundamentally a dualist while Freud was a strict materialist. For Jung there were two distinct worlds, the physical universe and the psychic world or universe. The laws of the psychic world, or to use Swedenborg's phrase, the spiritual world, were different and contrastive with the laws of the natural world. Jung realized that in the world of the mind or the psychic medium, "non-spatial images" had incalculable power and effect on the individual. Jung confesses that "instinct and spirit are beyond my understanding. They are terms which we posit for powerful forces whose nature we do not know." He contrasts his positive attitude towards religion with Freud's materialistic intolerance that leads him to ridicule the notion of

God as an unnecessary and neurotic emotional dependency rather than something real that we can interact with. Jung wrote:

> *My attitude to all religions is therefore a positive one. In their symbolism I recognize those figures which I have met with in the dreams and fantasies of my patients. In their moral teachings I see efforts that are the same as or similar to those made by my patients when, guided by their own insight or inspiration, they seek the right way to deal with the forces of psychic life. Ceremonial ritual, initiation rites, and ascetic practices, in all their forms and variations, interest me profoundly as so many techniques for bringing about a proper relation to these forces. My attitude to biology is equally positive, and to the empiricism of natural science in general, in which I see a herculean attempt to understand the psyche by approaching it from the outside world, just as religious gnosis is a prodigious attempt of the human mind to derive knowledge of the cosmos from within. In my picture of the world there is a vast outer realm and an equally vast inner realm; between these two stands man, facing now one and now the other, and, according to temperament and disposition, taking the one for the absolute truth by denying or sacrificing the other.* (Jung, in *Freud and Psychoanalysis*, 777)

> *In the darkness of the unconscious a treasure lies hidden, the same "treasure hard to attain" which in our text, and in many other places too, is described as the shining pearl, or, to quote Paracelsus, as the "mystery," by which is meant a fascinosum par excellence. It is these inherent possibilities of "spiritual" or "symbolic" life and of progress which form the ultimate, though unconscious, goal of regression. By serving as a means of expression, as bridges and pointers, symbols help to prevent the libido from getting stuck in the material corporeality of the mother. Never has the dilemma been more acutely formulated than in the Nicodemus dialogue: on the one hand the impossibility of entering again into the mother's womb; on the other, the need for rebirth from "water and spirit." The hero is a hero just because he sees resistance to the forbidden goal in all life's difficulties and yet fights that resistance with the whole-hearted yearning that strives towards the treasure hard to attain, and perhaps unattainable-a yearning that paralyses and kills the ordinary man.* (Jung, *Symbols of Transformation: The Dual Mother*, p. 511)

In general Jung tries to be conciliatory about his reputed differences with Freud but not in the area of the spiritual where Jung deplores Freud's materialism that binds him to biology and instinct as a theoretical dead end point. Jung marches on boldly exploring the ideas of religion and the spiritual as being inseparable properties of the psyche.

There is nothing that can free us from this bond except that opposite urge of life, the spirit. It is not the children of the flesh, but the "children of God/' who know freedom. In Ernst Barlach's tragedy The Dead Day, the mother-daemon says at the end: "The strange thing is that man will not learn that God is his father." That is what Freud would never learn, and what all those who share his out look forbid themselves to learn. At least, they never find the key to this knowledge. Theology does not help those who are looking for the key, because theology demands faith, and faith cannot be made: it is in the truest sense a gift of grace. We moderns are faced with the necessity of rediscovering the life of the spirit; we must experience it anew for ourselves. It is the only way in which to break the spell that binds us to the cycle of biological events.

My position on this question is the third point of difference between Freud's views and my own. Because of it I am accused of mysticism. I do not, however, hold myself responsible for the fact that man has, always and everywhere, spontaneously developed a religious function, and that the human psyche from time immemorial has been shot through with religious feelings and ideas. Whoever cannot see this aspect of the human psyche is blind, and whoever chooses to explain it away, or to "enlighten" it away, has no sense of reality. Or should we see in the father-complex which shows itself in all members of the Freudian school, and in its founder as well, evidence of a notable release from the fatalities of the family situation? This father complex, defended with such stubbornness and oversensitivity, is a religious function misunderstood, a piece of mysticism expressed in terms of biological and family relationships. As for Freud's concept of the "superego," it is a furtive attempt to smuggle the time-honoured image of Jehovah in the dress of psychological theory. For my part, I prefer to call things by the names under which they have always been known. (Jung, in *Freud and Psychoanalysis*, 781).

Unlike Freud drowning in materialistic biology and science, Jung calls for "the equal balance of the flesh and the spirit". Jung seems to say that to deny the spirit, as the Freudians do by ridiculing it, perpetuates neurosis and mental pathology in the individual. It is the spirit that balances out the flesh and gives individuals an opportunity of partaking in true humanity.

Jung attributes everything to the unconscious. The development of consciousness is dependent on the psychic forces that come out of the unconscious. "*What we see enacted on the stage of world-history happens also in the individual*" (ditto, 739). And as the individual matures in adulthood one becomes aware of "feelings of being secretly guided by otherworldly influences" (ditto). In his autobiography dictated in 1957 just before his death Jung reasserts once more that his entire work and life focus was not on the limited views that science can give, but on the expansive views that myth can give of the subjective, the personal, and the unique, and hence of what is really important and of value.

> *My life is a story of the self-realization of the unconscious. Everything in the unconscious seeks outward manifestation, and the personality too desires to evolve out of its unconscious conditions and to experience itself as a whole. I cannot employ the language of science to trace this process of growth in myself, for I cannot experience myself as a scientific problem. What we are to our inward vision, and what man appears to be sub specie aeternitatis, can only be expressed by way of myth. Myth is more individual and expresses life more precisely than does science. Science works with concepts of averages which are far too general to do justice to the subjective variety of an individual life. Thus it is that I have now undertaken, in my eighty-third year, to tell my personal myth. I can only make direct statements only "tell stories." Whether or not the stories are "true" is not the problem. The only question is whether what I tell is my fable, my truth. ...*
>
> *In the end the only events in my life worth telling are those when the imperishable world irrupted into this transitory one. That is why I speak chiefly of inner experiences, amongst which I include my dreams and visions. These form the prima materia of my scientific work. They were the fiery magma out of which the stone that had to be worked was crystallized.*
> (Jung, Memories, Dreams, Reflections, Prologue).

Weighted down by his self-imposed limitations of science Jung led a double life. One life was public, objective, empirical and not so important in the ultimate sense, as he states above. The other life was personal, subjective, and critically important. Jung struck a balance by inventing spiritual concepts that were collapsed and flattened into material definitions. For instance the spiritual idea of *synchronicity* was defined in natural observational terms as "meaningful or unusual coincidences" that one can observe in ordinary life. This simplex definition helped the adoption and spread of Jung's concept of synchronicity since everyone was able to think and come up with such examples in their lives.

In the years to come Jung's dualism will be more deeply explored by those who respond to his ideas. When this takes place Jung's influence will grow even more pervasively than it has in the first 100 years after his passing on.

Jung's Ideas on Immortality and Life After Death

Close to the end of his life on earth Jung states in his dictated or oral autobiography:

> *Six weeks after his death my father appeared to me in a dream. Suddenly he stood before me and said that he was coming back from his holiday. He had made a good recovery and was now coming home. I thought he would be annoyed with me for having moved into his room. But not a bit of it! Nevertheless, I felt ashamed because I had imagined he was dead. Two days later the dream was repeated. My father had recovered and was coming home, and again I reproached myself because I had thought he was dead. Later I kept asking myself: "What does it mean that my father returns in dreams and that he seems so real?" It was an unforgettable experience, and it forced me for the first time to think about life after death. (Jung, Memories, 123)*

What Jung's ideas were on life after death did not appear anywhere in his voluminous *Collected Works*. He talks about it at last at the end of his career just before passing on as an octogenarian. He made it a part of the agreement with the publisher to hold off publication until his death. Further, he asked that this book not be included in the collection known as Jung's *Collected Works*. The book's title is *Memories, Dreams, Reflections* (1961) and was edited and collected from a long series of recorded oral exchanges that he had with Aniela Jaffe, herself an expert analyst and long time friend of Jung. In her Introduction she reports that Jung agreed to call the book an "autobiography" but seemed reluctant to discuss his personal life beyond what he had presented in his books. In the end however he did go into that topic, and so we can now examine what were Jung's ideas about life after death.

> What I have to tell about the hereafter, and about life after death, consists entirely of memories, of images in which I have lived and of thoughts which have buffeted me. These memories in a way also underlie my works; for the latter are fundamentally nothing but attempts, ever renewed, to give an answer to the question of the interplay between the "here" and the "hereafter." Yet I have never written expressly about a life after death; for then I would have had to document my ideas, and I have no way of doing that. Be that as it may, I would like to state my ideas now. (Jung, Memories)

Here, as in in his much earlier book *Psychology and Religion*, Jung holds on to his never wavering purpose, which is to pursue spiritual matters only from an empirically objective approach. But now in his autobiography, which he insisted was to be published after his death, he relaxes his lifelong policy to discuss spiritual ideas only empirically as he had done in his book on *Psychology and Religion*. So now the voice of inner perception speaks out within him. Jung can now see and understand that dealing with spiritual ideas by phenomenological experience is consistent with an objective empirical and therefore scientific treatment of topics such as dreams, visions, and subtle perception. This is Jung's liberation at last from the tyranny of the negative bias in materialistic science, which he had inherited from Freud, and by which he was cowed all his life never to stray from.

Jung's inner spirit was suppressed and repressed for the sake of this career-oriented stricture. Freud gave Jung an early accolade, crowning him as his possible successor to the world of psychoanalysis. Jung played the role for the sake of his career, but the collegial relationship quickly ended when Jung started publishing his ideas about psychoanalysis, the psychic world, and the collective unconscious. Freud ejected and disbarred Jung's dualist ideas as inimical to psychoanalysis and to science.

Still, Jung seems to have been unable to shake himself free from Freud's kiss of death to Jung's spiritual leanings. Jung continued to immerse himself in the materialistic method of the negative bias science that was opposed to dualism and to all spiritual concepts, labeling them unscientific nonsense. It seems that once Jung was on his way in his career he had to continue playing the role of materialistic scientist. All of Jung's spiritual ideas and perceptions, real and clear as they were in his mind, had to be dressed up with the materialistic garb with its layering of physical measurement. It was a giant benevolent fraud perpetrated on the tyrants of science, like Freud and many others that followed. They did their best to enforce a professional policy of *intellectual tyranny*. They instituted threatening strictures to fire scientists from their rank if they did not pay homage to the negative bias, to monism, to anti-dualism, to materialism, to atheism. It is a historical irony that psychology's turn to behaviorism in the second half the twentieth century upheld Freud's work as the quintessential example of unscientific and subjective psychology that should be ridiculed and avoided.

This climate of scientific intolerance of dualism characterizes all of psychology in the twentieth century. The advent of the "phenomenological approach" in the midst of this negative bias climate did not in fact depart from materialism. The strict requirement of empiricism did not allow phenomenological research to leave the flatness of earth and its sense-bound perception and reasoning. Dualism in science could not be born in such a hostile climate. Jung's insight and perception into spiritual topics remained private in his own mind as he went through the decades of publishing about "psychic" topics. By the time Jung arrived to his old age there was a great gap between what he had written in his books and what he understood about spiritual topics.

Unknown to his readers, followers, and critics was the fact that Jung's entire life work was focused around one center, which was "*to give an answer to the question of the interplay between the "here" and the "hereafter*" (Jung, *Memories*). This astonishing personal disclosure puts Jung's work in a new historical context for psychology.

It is common in psychology to present Jung's works in a context of agnosticism. You do not have to be a dualist or theist to use Jung's work as a psychotherapist or psychiatrist, nor in the psychology of personal development. This is clearly the result of Jung's lifelong professional attitude not to go beyond the empirical and the objective in discussing psychic matters. And so now it is quite another thing to read or reread Jung's works from this new context, which is not agnostic but dualist, spiritual, and theistic.

Perhaps one has to be close to death to acquire the necessary freedom to talk about it. It is not that I wish we had a life after death. In fact, I would prefer not to foster such ideas. Still, I must state, to give reality its due, that, without my wishing and without my doing anything about it, thoughts of this nature move about within me. I can't say whether these thoughts are true or false, but I do know they are there, and can be given utterance, if I do not repress them out of some prejudice. Prejudice cripples and injures the full phenomenon of psychic life. . (Jung, Memories)

Even here Jung does not abandon his lack of enthusiasm for a life after death and in fact reasserts his preference "*not to foster such ideas*". Why not, one may ask, if he believes it to be part of human reality and psychology? It remains unclear how much Jung had read of Swedenborg fifty years earlier when he had been a medical student at the university, and how much information he may have remembered from it given that he is silent on Swedenborg's spiritual ideas in Jung's *Collected Works* except for two minor references. If he laid Swedenborg aside for fifty years, one may suppose that Jung was unaware of Swedenborg's detailed descriptions of the resuscitation of the dead that Swedenborg obtained from hundreds of direct empirical observations of people dying and being resuscitated, including himself.

Mythic-Emotional Man
vs. Scientific-Intellect Man

We cannot visualize another world ruled by quite other laws, the reason being that we live in a specific world which has helped to shape our minds and establish our basic psychic conditions. We are strictly limited by our innate structure and therefore bound by our whole being and thinking to this world of ours. Mythic man, to be sure, demands a "going beyond all that" but scientific man cannot permit this. To the intellect, all my mythologizing is futile speculation. To the emotions however, it is a healing and valid activity; it gives existence a glamour which we would not like to do without. Nor is there any good reason why we should. (~Carl Jung, Memories)

Visible here is Jung's lifelong split between the life of our intellect and the emotional life. He identifies the intellect with "scientific man" while the "mythic man" is identified with "going beyond" what is merely of this world, thus dualism. In the light of Swedenborg's work we can clarify this personality split as normal rather than dissociated or schizoid. If the split were abnormal then scientific man in the personality and mythic man would work against each other. In that case people would develop personality types that emphasize one or the other since the two are not compatible.

When these two types of personality functions are defined as incompatible, it gives rise to the idea that there are two different types of people. The intellect-scientific type person sticks to materialism and wants to reject dualism and theism, thus God and life after death. The emotional-mythic type person senses the other-worldliness of our experience and existence, and hence looks favorably to the idea of life after death in an all-encompassing psychic world of the collective unconscious.

Jung's work has fostered this kind of schizoid split in twentieth-century materialist psychology. But as will be seen next there is no actual split of this sort in people's personality structure. Intellectual or "scientific man" can find rational theory and empirical fact about the spiritual world of eternity, also known as the afterlife. This makes sense since the afterlife is in the spiritual world, and a "world" implies the existence of events and objects, and these constitute empirical objective data through perceptual input. There is no actual opposition between the spiritual and the rational as is shown throughout this book, and in fact it is the interior unconscious spiritual-rational function in human thinking that makes possible the exterior lower function of the natural-rational intellect of science.

Neither is there an opposition between the intellectual and the emotional functions in our thinking. Anatomy indicates that the lungs cannot respire without the inflow of oxygenated blood. There is no respiratory function without blood circulation. In a correspondent way affective functions in the mind cannot operate without cognitive functions, and vice versa. If the motivational and intentional system of the mind shuts down, there is no further thinking and planning taking place. Every act of thinking needs a motive or else it ceases. It follows that emotions cannot exist without thoughts. Experiencing emotions is an affective function that is closely connected to motivation and sensation or pleasure and pain. If the affective functions together with the cognitive, and cannot be separated in functioning, then it's clear that "emotional man" is an integral part of "scientific man" and vice versa.

In Swedenborg this dilemma is fully resolved. There are two levels of intellectual ideas and thinking. One type of mental functioning is lower or external and is called "natural-rational" consciousness. It is based on input from the physical senses, and hence on concepts that are based on physical measurement and physical time-space properties. This is the "scientific man" that Jung identifies as being opposed to what is spiritual (or "mythical"), opposed to dualism and to theism.

The rational mind, or rational level of functioning is active at two discrete levels of complexity. The lower level is exterior anatomically and may be called the *natural*-rational level of functioning. The higher level is interior anatomically and may be called "*spiritual*-rational" consciousness. Jung may have exerted a prejudiced influence on his followers by leaving this split between the intellect and the emotions as permanent in human consciousness, and thus leading to the idea of a contrastive personality type that does not in fact exist in human personality. The result is that some people identify themselves as "emotional", "mythical" or "spiritual" exclusively, and therefore try to reject the intellectual and scientific from their mental structure. But this is an error as can be seen from what follows, namely, that the scientific and the emotional/affective components of personality are part of the mental structure of every individual. Unless both are present and function together, human growth cannot proceed normally. It is likely that Jung himself realized that there is no actual split in personality type, but that he allowed this impression for professional and political reasons. It was clear to him from his own mental development that these two types are phases of growth in which the higher not yet realized aspect is denied by the lower, but that these are only appearances.

The view from Swedenborg is that *natural*-rational consciousness is opposed to the *spiritual*-rational consciousness only to begin with, but not later when the individual's consciousness of the spiritual opens up with psychological and intellectual development. This mental growth process is called "regeneration" by which an individual comes to realize that the authentic spiritual life can grow only in a personality that is focused on acquiring moral behavior as a prerequisite to spiritual development and eternal happiness. Human beings first acquire a sensuous-material consciousness in childhood, and this is followed in adolescence and young adulthood by a natural-rational consciousness that results from experience, knowledge, and science becoming part of one's attitude and reasoning.

The mythical is not actually the counterpart of the intellectual, as Jung had initially proposed, except when mythic man remains at the level of superstition and mystery, which belongs to the unregenerate natural consciousness. But if mythic man moves on to experiencing regeneration and moral character change, then dualism and theism become present in the mind as the experiencing of *spiritual*-rational consciousness. In Swedenborg we can clearly see that the higher spiritual-rational consciousness that evolves with regeneration is actually a purified and superior rational and intellectual. This higher consciousness is not the emotional, as Jung initially proposed. Instead, spiritual is rational, and we may use the expression "spiritual-rational" thinking to contrast with the lower "natural-rational" thinking. All of the spiritual concepts introduced by Swedenborg – and there are hundreds – are purely rational in thinking and reasoning.

For instance, with respect to religion, Swedenborg argues that there is no psychological advantage to a so-called "blind faith" that relies on obscure mysticism or unfathomable mystery. Swedenborg's exposition exhibits the empirical rationality of the concepts of God, *Sacred Scripture*, the afterlife, eternity, heaven and hell, spirits, angels, good, evil, truth, infinity, omnipresence, etc. Those who are "emotional" in personality type without being intellectual and rational are limited to *natural*-rational reasoning, and cannot comprehend the meanings of any of these spiritual ideas. When they attempt to comprehend them, the result is denial and rejection of anything that is immaterial and belonging to the spiritual world or realm. But in *spiritual*-rational understanding Swedenborg's ideas are rationalized and demystified. They provide certainty about life after death and clarity about its determining relationship to the individual's personality development.

Jung wrote about the advantages of spiritual-rational consciousness by which we can perceive that our life has *"indefinite continuity"*, that is, that we are immortal.

> *Leaving aside the rational arguments against any certainty in these matters, we must not forget that for most people it means a great deal to assume that their lives will have an indefinite continuity beyond their present existence. They live more sensibly, feel better, and are more at peace. One has*

centuries, one has an inconceivable period of time at one's disposal. What then is the point of this senseless mad rush? (Jung, Memories)

Here Jung is talking about immortality. This statement puts Jung fully into the dualist camp of thinking. From the perspective of his own spiritual-rational consciousness Jung can clearly see that it makes all the difference to people whether they think of themselves as immortal or mortal. To think of ourselves as immortal means to have "*an indefinite continuity beyond our present existence*". When time is lifted there is no pressure of time. We can give up "*this senseless mad rush*" which is caused by time running out.

According to Jung the "*decisive and telling question*" for human beings is whether we are "*related to something infinite or not*". When we realize that "*the thing which truly matters is the infinite*" then we can avoid "futilities" and other "limitations" that rob us from life's real satisfactions. Life is felt as "*limited*" because our goals are limited to "*false possessions*" rather than "*essentials*". The result is the consciousness of living with "*envy and jealousy*", which is a "*life wasted*". This element of "*boundlessness*" needs to be expressed and realized in our interactions with others. In this struggle for meaning the "*self*" furnishes our "*greatest limitation*" because it robs our consciousness from a "*link to the limitlessness of the unconscious*".

Ego-Consciousness and the Unconscious

Jung perceived that the function of myth and religious symbolism in human thinking is to help the conscious come into the limitless knowledges of the unconscious. He referred to this as the "union of the conscious and the unconscious". The understanding that is possible in the unconscious is of a higher order, as was discussed above regarding the contrast between merely *natural*-rational thinking and the elevated *spiritual*-rational thinking. Spiritual understanding becomes perceptible to natural consciousness when the two act together rather than in opposition to each other. The prejudice of materialism prevents access to spiritual information. Jung saw that the unconscious is "*the generator of the empirical personality*". This led him to the conclusion that "*our unconscious existence is the real one and our conscious world a kind of illusion*".

The conscious intellect presents only an "*apparent reality constructed for a specific purpose*" by the actual reality, which is the unconscious. Jung came to realize that "*man's task is to become conscious of the contents that press upward from the unconscious*", and that "*his destiny is to create more and more consciousness*".

> Myth is the natural and indispensable intermediate stage between unconscious and conscious cognition. True, the unconscious knows more than consciousness does; but it is knowledge of a special sort, knowledge in eternity, usually without reference to the here and now, not couched in language of the intellect. Only when we let its statements amplify themselves, as has been shown above by the example of numerals, does it come within the range of our understanding; only then does a new aspect become perceptible to us. This process is convincingly repeated in every successful dream analysis. That is why it is so important not to have any preconceived, doctrinaire opinions about the statements made by dreams. As soon as a certain "monotony of interpretation" strikes us, we know that our approach has become doctrinaire and hence sterile. (Jung, *Memories, Dreams, Reflections*, 390)

Jung sees that in psychotherapy the "language of the intellect" that has become stale, doctrinaire, and prejudiced is immersed in material consciousness, time-bound, place-bound and measurement-bound. What is needed is an enlightened intellect that is elevated above the darkness of the mere physical. This is spiritual consciousness, which is far above the material, the sensuous, and the prejudiced. It is not the intellect that hinders superior consciousness since there is no other venue for consciousness then the awareness of reality and rationality, thus of the intellect. The higher intellect is what looks down on the lower intellect when the individual enters spiritual consciousness through regeneration. The struggle between going down to material consciousness or going up to spiritual consciousness is ever present in the human mind. In the following extract this struggle between up and down, or inward and outward, is dramatically enacted in two vivid dreams that Jung reports.

One night I lay awake thinking of the sudden death of a friend whose funeral had taken place the day before. I was deeply concerned. Suddenly I felt that he was in the room. It seemed to me that he stood at the foot of my bed and was asking me to go with him. I did not have the feeling of an apparition; rather, it was an inner visual image of him, which I explained to myself as a fantasy. But in all honesty I had to ask myself, "Do I have any proof that this is a fantasy? Suppose it is not a fantasy, suppose my friend is really here and I decided he was only a fantasy would that not be abominable of me?" Yet I had equally little proof that he stood before me as an apparition. Then I said to myself, "Proof is neither here nor there! Instead of explaining him away as a fantasy, I might just as well give him the benefit of the doubt and for experiment's sake credit him with reality." The moment I had that thought, he went to the door and beckoned me to follow him. So I was going to have to play along with him! That was something I hadn't bargained for. I had to repeat my argument to myself once more. Only then did I follow him in my imagination.

He led me out of the house, into the garden, out to the road, and finally to his house, (In reality it was several hundred yards away from mine.) I went in, and he conducted me into his study. He climbed on a stool and showed me the second of five books with red bindings which stood on the second shelf from the top. Then the vision broke off. I was not acquainted with his library and did not know what books he owned. Certainly I could never have made out from below the titles of the books he had pointed out to me on the second shelf from the top.

This experience seemed to me so curious that next morning I went to his widow and asked whether I could look up something in my friend's library. Sure enough, there was a stool standing under the bookcase I had seen in my vision, and even before I came closer I could see the five books with red bindings. I stepped up on the stool so as to be able to read the titles. They were translations of the novels of Emile Zola. The title of the second volume read: "The Legacy of the Dead." The contents seemed to me of no interest. Only the title was extremely significant in connection with this experience.

Jung is caught in the gap between natural and spiritual consciousness. The lower form says this is a fantasy. The higher form says this is real. It should be noted that Jung never mixes the physical and the spiritual or psychic. Some people who discuss this subject seem to think that their physical eyes can see spiritual beings or objects, and this is impossible by definition. Physical things can relate only to other physical things, and never to mental things. When we think of moving the fingers and pick up something the physical reacts to the mental by built in correspondence. There is no direct contact possible between the physical and the spiritual. The two can interact only by correspondence. Jung knew this and his descriptions of encounters with spirits were always in the mental world, in the dream, or in the imagination.

I had dreamed once before of the problem of the self and the ego. In that earlier dream I was on a hiking trip. I was walking along a little road through a hilly landscape; the sun was shining and I had a wide view in all directions. Then I came to a small wayside chapel. The door was ajar, and I went in. To my surprise there was no image of the Virgin on the altar, and no crucifix either, but only a wonderful flower arrangement. But then I saw that on the floor in front of the altar, facing me, sat a yogi in lotus posture, in deep meditation. When I looked at him more closely, I realized that he had my face.

I started in profound fright, and awoke with the thought: "Aha, so he is the one who is meditating me. He has a dream, and I am it." I knew that when he awakened, I would no longer be. I had this dream after my illness in 1944. It is a parable: My self retires into meditation and meditates my earthly form. To put it another way: it assumes human shape in order to enter three dimensional existence, as if someone were putting on a diver's suit in order to dive into the sea. When it renounces existence in the hereafter, the self assumes a religious posture, as the chapel in the dream shows. In earthly form it can pass through the experiences of the three-dimensional world, and by greater awareness take a further step toward realization. (p. 388)

But closer study shows that as a rule the images of the unconscious are not produced by consciousness, but have a reality and spontaneity of their own, Nevertheless, we regard them as mere marginal phenomena. (...)

The aim of both these dreams is to effect a reversal of the relationship between ego-consciousness and the unconscious, and to represent the unconscious as the generator of the empirical personality. This reversal suggests that in the opinion of the "other side," our unconscious existence is the real one and our conscious world a kind of illusion, an apparent reality constructed for a specific purpose, like a dream which seems a reality as long as we are in it. It is clear that this state of affairs resembles very closely the Oriental conception of Maya. Unconscious wholeness therefore seems to me the true spiritus rector of all biological and psychic events. Here is a principle which strives for total realization which in man's case signifies the attainment of total consciousness. Attainment of consciousness is culture in the broadest sense, and self-knowledge is therefore the heart and essence of this process. The Oriental attributes unquestionably divine significance to the self, and according to the ancient Christian view self-knowledge is the road to knowledge of God. (Jung, *Memories, Dreams, Reflections*, 390)

We can see here Jung's radical counterproposal for psychology as conceptualized by Freud and other dynamic theorists. There is need for a *"reversal of the relationship between ego-consciousness and the unconscious, and to represent the unconscious as the generator of the empirical personality"*. It is the spiritual consciousness to which we aspire that actually creates the material consciousness of our daily lives. It is not the lower that rises to the higher, but the higher lowers itself to the lower and infuses it with a new superior consciousness.

When the unconscious is in the conscious spiritual enlightenment takes place. The spiritual-rational meanings in the natural-rational understanding create the self-knowledge, and consequently self-realization. The material without the spiritual in it appears as an illusion. It provides only an apparent reality to fit one's desires and prejudices. The result is individual suffering and incompleteness.

The method of discipline by which the merely material consciousness can be infilled with spiritual consciousness is the method of regeneration or individuation. This method cuts through the illusions that captivate the material consciousness. Individuation through self-knowledge is possible because the future self is already present in the unconscious. The self grows as this future enters the conscious and becomes the present by application.

Jung Discovers
the Writings of Swedenborg

When Jung was doing his medical university studies he naturally started reading about science and philosophy topics. But we need to realize that he had already decided he was a dualist and thought of the psyche as a separate world. Jung had come to this position already as a teenager and now he was looking for *scientific* confirmation. He did not find it in the materialism of science. Nor did he find it in the intellectual world outside the scientific community. He marveled at the inability of people in mere natural consciousness to think with meaning about dualist concepts such as life after death or a psychic world that existed apart from the physical and what belonged to physical time, space, and measurement. Such spiritual ideas evoked "dread" in other people and Jung wondered why.

During my first years at the university I made the discovery that while science opened the door to enormous quantities of knowledge, it provided genuine insights very sparingly, and these in the main were of a specialized nature. I knew from my philosophical reading that the existence of the psyche was responsible for this situation. Without the psyche there would be neither knowledge nor insight. Yet nothing was ever said about the psyche. Everywhere it was tacitly taken for granted, and even when someone mentioned it--as did C. G. Carus, for example-- there was no real knowledge of it but only philosophical speculation which might just as easily take one turn as another. I could make neither head nor tail of this curious observation.

At the end of my second semester, however, I made another discovery, which was to have great consequences. In the library of a classmate's father I came upon a small book on spiritualistic phenomena, dating from the seventies. It was an account of beginnings of spiritualism, and was written by a theologian. My initial doubts were quickly dissipated, for I could not help seeing that the phenomena described in the book were in principle much the same as the stories I had heard again and again in the country since my earliest childhood. The material, without a doubt, was authentic. But the great question of whether these stories were physically true was not answered to my satisfaction.

Nevertheless, it could be established that at all times and all over the world the same stories had been reported again and again. There must be some reason for this, and it could not possibly have been the predominance of the same religious conceptions everywhere, for that was obviously not the case. Rather it must be connected with the objective behavior of the human psyche. But with regard to this cardinal question--the objective nature of the psyche--I could find out absolutely nothing, except what the philosophers said. (Jung, *Memories*, 126)

My mother's No. 2 sympathized wholeheartedly with my enthusiasm, but everyone else I knew was distinctly discouraging. Hitherto I had encountered only the brick wall of traditional views, but now I came up against the steel of people's prejudice and their utter incapacity to admit unconventional possibilities. I found this even with my closest friends. To them all this was far worse than my preoccupation with theology. I had the feeling that I had pushed to the brink of the world; what was of burning interest to me was null and void for others, and even a cause for dread.

Dread of what? I could find no explanation for this. After all, there was nothing preposterous or world-shaking in the idea that there might be events which overstepped the limited categories of space, time, and causality (Jung, *Memories*, 127)

It is clear from these remarks that Jung and Freud would never be able to work together. Their enthusiasm for each other at the beginning could only endure for so long as Jung remained silent about his actual ideas. Freud was a passionate atheist and totally sold on materialism and reductionism in psychology. As it turns out, Freud and Jung were intellectual opposites, thus inner enemies. This also applies to their ideas so that whatever Freud contributed and still does to psychology, Jung contributes the annihilation of those ideas. Material consciousness such as that in which are immersed the ideas of Freud, appears deflated and lifeless in the view of spiritual-rational consciousness, as were the ideas of Jung and Swedenborg.

It is around this time of his schooling that Jung read some works by Swedenborg. It is noteworthy that Jung's knowledge of Swedenborg was not made part of the large body of Jung's writings except as a few minor references to Swedenborg's reputed "clairvoyance". It is my view that Jung, like Kant before him, took care not to injure his professional reputation as a scientist by revealing that his ideas are closely allied to a man considered to be a mystic and visionary theologian. Only at the very end of his career did Jung at last acknowledge that he had been a dualist all along and that Swedenborg's writings sustained Jung through his most difficult struggles in the progression of his psychic development.

But because Jung kept Swedenborg away from his psychology, the psychic world remained in Jung's work shrouded in an impenetrable *shadow* of obscurity and indefiniteness. Instead of the empirical clarity of Swedenborg's ethnography of the psychic world of the afterlife, Jung had to settle for other evidence, much less direct and certain, such as religious symbolism and dreams. Jung's certainty of a life after death was partly based on his spiritual consciousness while dreaming. The experiencing of his dreams was one of Jung's empirical foundation.

> Not only my own dreams, but also occasionally the dreams of others, helped to shape, revise, or confirm my views on a life after death. I attach particular importance to a dream which a pupil of mine, a woman of sixty, dreamed about two months before her death. She had entered the hereafter. There was a class going on, and various deceased women friends of hers sat on the front bench. An atmosphere of general expectation prevailed. She looked around for a teacher or lecturer, but could find none. Then it became plain that she herself was the lecturer, for immediately after death people had to give accounts of the total experience of their lives. The dead were extremely interested in the life experiences that the newly deceased brought with them, just as if the acts and experiences taking place in earthly life, in space and time, were the decisive ones. (Jung, Memories)

It is quite remarkable that Jung had the idea that "immediately after death people had to give accounts of the total experience of their lives" -- which accords with the factual reports of Swedenborg. Also, that "the dead were extremely interested in the life experiences that the newly deceased brought with them".

The following is a description from Swedenborg's ethnography that is concordant with Jung's conclusions. A summary is provided at the end of the extract. Swedenborg uses the word "spirits" to refer to people in the afterlife after awakening from the two-day dying-resuscitation process. He uses the expression "angels" and "devils" to refer to people in a later stage when they enter the mental state of either heaven or hell.

Swedenborg's Near Death Experiences

The Resuscitation Of Man From The Dead
And His Entrance Into Eternal Life (by Swedenborg)

When the body is no longer able to perform the bodily functions in the natural world that correspond to the spirit's thoughts and affections, which the spirit has from the spiritual world, man is said to die. This takes place when the respiration of the lungs and the beatings of the heart cease. But the man does not die; he is merely separated from the bodily part that was of use to him in the world, while the man himself continues to live. It is said that the man himself continues to live since man is not a man because of his body but because of his spirit, for it is the spirit that thinks in man, and thought with affection is what constitutes man. Evidently, then, the death of man is merely his passing from one world into another. And this is why in the Word in its internal sense "death" signifies resurrection and continuation of life.

There is an inmost communication of the spirit with the breathing and with the beating of the heart, the spirit's thought communicating with the breathing, and its affection, which is of love, with the heart; 446-1 consequently when these two motions cease in the body there is at once a separation. These two motions, the respiration of the lungs and the beating of heart, are the very bond on the sundering of which the spirit is left to itself; and the body being then deprived of the life of its spirit grows cold and begins to decay. This inmost communication of the spirit of man is with the respiration and with the heart, because on these all vital motions depend, not only in general but in every particular.

After the separation the spirit of man continues in the body for a short time, but only until the heart's action has wholly ceased, which happens variously in accord with the diseased condition that causes death, with some the motion of the heart continuing for some time, with others not so long. As soon as this motion ceases the man is resuscitated; but this is done by the Lord alone. Resuscitation means the drawing forth of the spirit from the body, and its introduction into the spiritual world; this is commonly called the resurrection. The spirit is not separated from the body until the motion of the heart has ceased, for the reason that the heart corresponds to the affection of love, which is the very life of man, for it is from love that everyone has vital heat; 447-1 consequently as long as this conjunction continues correspondence continues, and thereby the life of the spirit in the body.

How this resuscitation is effected has both been told to me and shown to me in living experience. The actual experience was granted to me that I might have a complete knowledge of the process.

As to the senses of the body I was brought into a state of insensibility, thus nearly into the state of the dying; but with the interior life and thought remaining unimpaired, in order that I might perceive and retain in the memory the things that happened to me, and that happen to those that are resuscitated from the dead. I perceived that the respiration of the body was almost wholly taken away; but the interior respiration of the spirit went on in connection with a slight and tacit respiration of the body. Then at first a communication of the pulse of the heart with the celestial kingdom was established, because that kingdom corresponds to the heart in man. Angels from that kingdom were seen, some at a distance, and two sitting near my head. Thus all my own affection was taken away although thought and perception continued.

I was in this state for some hours. Then the spirits that were around me withdrew, thinking that I was dead; and an aromatic odor like that of an embalmed body was perceived, for when the celestial angels are present everything pertaining to the corpse is perceived as aromatic, and when spirits perceive this they cannot approach; and in this way evil spirits are kept away from man's spirit when he is being introduced into eternal life. The angels seated at my head were silent, merely sharing their thoughts with mine; and when their thoughts are received the angels know that the spirit of man is in a state in which it can be drawn forth from the body. This sharing of their thoughts was effected by looking into my face, for in this way in heaven thoughts are shared.

As my thought and perception continued, that I might know and remember how resuscitation is effected, I perceived the angels first tried to ascertain what my thought was, whether it was like the thought of those who are dying, which is usually about eternal life; also that they wished to keep my mind in that thought. Afterwards I was told that the spirit of man is held in its last thought when the body expires, until it returns to the thoughts that are from its general or ruling affection in the world. Especially was I permitted to see and feel that there was a pulling and drawing forth, as it were, of the interiors of my mind, thus of my spirit, from the body; and I was told that this is from the Lord, and that the resurrection is thus effected.

The celestial angels who are with the one that is resuscitated do not withdraw from him, because they love everyone; but when the spirit comes into such a state that he can no longer be affiliated with celestial angels, he longs to get away from them. When this takes place angels from the Lord's spiritual kingdom come, through whom is given the use of light; for before this he saw nothing, but merely thought. I was shown how this is done. The angels appeared to roll off, as it were, a coat from the left eye towards the bridge of the nose, that the eye might be opened and be enabled to see. This is only an appearance, but to the spirit it seemed to be really done.

When the coat thus seems to have been rolled off there is a slight sense of light, but very dim, like what is seen through the eyelids on first awakening from sleep. To me this dim light took on a heavenly hue, but I was told afterwards that the color varies. Then something is felt to be gently rolled off from the face, and when this is done spiritual thought is awakened. This rolling off from the face is also an appearance, which represents the spirit's passing from natural thought into spiritual thought. The angels are extremely careful that only such ideas as savor of love shall proceed from the one resuscitated. They now tell him that he is a spirit.

When he has come into the enjoyment of light the spiritual angels render to the new spirit every service he can possibly desire in that state; and teach him about the things of the other life so far as he can comprehend them. But if he has no wish to be taught the spirit longs to get away from the company of the angels. Nevertheless, the angels do not withdraw from him, but he separates himself from them; for the angels love everyone, and desire nothing so much as to render service, to teach, and to lead into heaven; this constitutes their highest delight. When the spirit has thus withdrawn he is received by good spirits, and as long as he continues in their company everything possible is done for him.

But if he had lived such a life in the world as would prevent his enjoying the company of the good he longs to get away from the good, and this experience is repeated until he comes into association with such as are in entire harmony with his life in the world; and with such he finds his own life, and what is surprising, he then leads a life like that which he led in the world. (Swedenborg, *Heaven and Hell*, 445)

Swedenborg's experience of the dying-resuscitation process is discussed below in the last section in connection with Jung's account of his near death experiences.

Regarding the phase that immediately follows the dying-resuscitation process Swedenborg makes these clarifications:

> It shall first be explained what a spirit is, and what an angel is. All persons after death come, in the first place, into the world of spirits, which is midway between heaven and hell, and there pass through their own times, that is, their own states, and become prepared, according to their life, either for heaven or for hell. So long as people stay in that world they are called spirits. They who have been raised out of that world into heaven are called angels; but those who have been cast down into hell are called either satans or devils.

> So long as these continue in the world of spirits, those who are preparing for heaven are called angelic spirits; and those who are preparing for hell, infernal spirits; meanwhile angelic spirits are conjoined with heaven, and infernal spirits with hell. All spirits in the world of spirits are adjoined to people still on earth; because people still on earth, in respect to the interiors of their minds, are in like manner between heaven and hell, and through these spirits they communicate with heaven or with hell according to their life. It is to be observed that the world of spirits is one thing, and the spiritual world another; the world of spirits is that which has just been spoken of; but the spiritual world includes that world, and heaven and hell. (Swedenborg, Divine Love and Wisdom 140)

> All who come into the other life are vastated [=psychological process of anatomical purification]. Those who have been in good, in the world, are vastated as to evils and the falsities thence arising; and they are, then, in their own good and in the truth then arising. But those who have been in evil, are vastated as to truths and goods, if they have any; and they are, then, in their own evil and in the falsity arising from it. Hence, the good become images of their own good, and the evil, images of their own evil. The latter are, thus, cast down into hell; the former are raised up to heaven. (Swedenborg, Spiritual Experiences 5071)

All the speech of spirits and of angels is also effected by means of representatives; for by wonderful variations of light and shade they vividly present before the internal and at the same time before the external sight of him with whom they speak, all they are thinking about, and insinuate it by suitable changes of the state of the affections. The representations that come forth in such speech are not like those before described, but are quick and instantaneous, being simultaneous with the ideas that belong to their speech. They are like something that is described in a long series, while at the same time it is exhibited in an image before the eyes, for, wonderful to say, all spiritual things themselves whatever can be representatively exhibited by forms of imagery that are incomprehensible to man, within which are things of the perception of truth, and still more interiorly those of the perception of good.

Such things are also in man (for man is a spirit clothed with a body); as is evident from the fact that all speech perceived by the ear, on ascending toward the interiors, passes into forms [ideas] not unlike those of sight, and from these into intellectual forms or ideas, and thus becomes a perception of the sense of the expressions. Whoever rightly reflects upon these things may know from them that there is in himself a spirit which is his internal man, and also that after the separation of the body he will possess such a speech, because he is in the very same during his life in the world, although it does not appear to him that he is in it, by reason of the obscurity and darkness which earthly, bodily, and worldly things induce. (Swedenborg, Arcana Coelestia 3342)

Regarding his dual consciousness and mission the following statements by Swedenborg are informative:

I anticipate that many who read the following descriptions and the accounts at the ends of the succeeding chapters will believe they are figments of my imagination. I swear in truth, however, that they are not inventions, but actual occurrences to which I was witness. Nor were they witnessed in any condition of unconsciousness but in a state of full wakefulness. For it has pleased the Lord to manifest Himself to me and send me to teach the doctrines that will be doctrines of the New Church, the church meant by the New Jerusalem in the book of Revelation. To this end He has opened the inner faculties of my mind and spirit. As a result, it has been made possible for me to be in the spiritual world with angels and at the same time in the natural world with men, and this now for twenty-five years. (Swedenborg, Conjugial Love 1)

In the chapter on the Sacred Scripture I showed that the literal sense of the Word is written by appearances and correspondences. Each of its details therefore contains a spiritual sense in which truth is illuminated by its own light, and the literal sense is in shadow. So to prevent the people of the new church, like those of the old church, going astray in the shadows obscuring the literal sense of the Word, especially as regards heaven and hell, how they will live after death, and on the present occasion about the Lord's coming, the Lord has been pleased to open the sight of my spirit, thus admitting me to the spiritual world.

I have been allowed not only to talk with spirits and angels, with relations and friends, even with kings and princes, who have met their end in the natural world, but also to see the astonishing sights of heaven, and the pitiful sights of hell. So I have seen how people do not pass their time in some pu deep in the earth, nor flit around blind and dumb in the air or in empty space, but live as human beings in a substantial body, in a much more perfect state, if they come among the blessed, than they experienced previously when living in material bodies. (Swedenborg, The True Christian Religion 771).

So long as man lives in the world, he is kept midway between heaven and hell, and is there in spiritual equilibrium, which is freedom of choice.

In order to know what freedom of choice is and the nature of it, it is necessary to know its origin. Especially from a recognition of its origin it can be known, not only that there is such a thing as freedom of choice, but also what it is. Its origin is in the spiritual world, where man's mind is kept by the Lord. Man's mind is his spirit, which lives after death; and his spirit is constantly in company with its like in the spiritual world, and at the same time by means of the material body with which it is enveloped, it is with men in the natural world.

Man does not know that in respect to his mind he is in the midst of spirits, for the reason that the spirits with whom he is in company in the spiritual world, think and speak spiritually, while his own spirit thinks and speaks naturally so long as he is in the material body; and the natural man cannot understand or perceive spiritual thought and speech, nor the reverse. This is why spirits cannot be seen. (Swedenborg, The True Christian Religion 475).

Jung Communicates
With the Departed

It is noteworthy that Jung identified the "spirits of the departed" with the "figures of the unconscious" that appeared to him psychically and engaged in communication with him. In his book *Psychology and Religion* written decades before his autobiography Jung had interactions with the spirits who were his "forefathers":

> Quite early I had learned that it was necessary for me to instruct the figures of the unconscious, or that other group which is often indistinguishable from them, the "spirits of the departed." The first time I experienced this was on a bicycle trip through upper Italy which I took with a friend in 1911. (Jung, p. 379) ...

> Not until years later did I understand the dream and my reaction. The bewigged gentleman was a kind of ancestral spirit, or spirit of the dead, who had addressed questions to me in vain! It was still too soon, I had not yet come so far, but I had an obscure feeling that by working on my book I would be answering the question that had been asked. It had been asked by, as it were, my spiritual forefathers, in the hope and expectation that they would learn what they had not been able to find out during their time on earth, since the answer had first to be created in the centuries that followed. If question and answer had already been in existence in eternity, had always been there, no effort on my part would have been necessary, and it could all have been discovered in any other century. There seems to be unlimited knowledge present in nature, it is true, but it can be comprehended by consciousness only when the time is ripe for it. The process, presumably, is like what happens in the individual psyche: a man may go about for many years with an inkling of something, but grasps it clearly only at a particular moment. (Jung, *Memories, Dreams, Reflections*, p. 379)

The passage above is a good indication of how seriously Jung took his conversations with the spirits of his forefathers. He supposed that they were asking him questions about things they did not know having been away from contact with earth for centuries and living in the eternity of the collective conscious. What to Jung was the collective unconscious, to the departed who were in it was the collective conscious. Jung concluded from this that even though all knowledge is contained in the collective unconscious it is not accessible to the conscious until we are ready to appear there.

> Later, when I wrote the *Septem Sermones ad Mortuos*, once again it was the dead who addressed crucial questions to me. They came so they said "back from Jerusalem, where they found not what they sought." This had surprised me greatly at the time, for according to the traditional views the dead are the possessors of great knowledge. People have the idea that the dead know far more than we, for Christian doctrine teaches that in the hereafter we shall "see face to face." Apparently, however, the souls of the dead "know" only what they knew at the moment of death, and nothing beyond that. Hence their endeavor to penetrate into life in order to share in the knowledge of men. I frequently have a feeling that they are standing directly behind us, waiting to hear what answer we will give to them, and what answer to destiny. It seems to me as if they were dependent on the living for receiving answers to their questions, that is, on those who have survived them and exist in a world of change: as if omniscience or, as I might put it, omni-consciousness, were not at their disposal, but could flow only into the psyche of the living, into a soul bound to a body. The mind of the living appears, therefore, to hold an advantage over that of the dead in at least one point: in the capacity for attaining clear and decisive cognitions. (Jung, *Memories, Dreams, Reflections*, p. 371)

In the quote above Jung concludes that the departed spirits *"endeavor to penetrate into life in order to share in the knowledge of men"*. Swedenborg confirms from much observation in dual consciousness that people in the other life, called spirits, intensely desire to connect with people on earth in a conscious way as in a dialogue. If they achieve this with someone, the spirits are then able to sense through the individual and to see, hear, or move as they wish, thus taking over the will of the person. Swedenborg states that this kind of "spirit possession" was actual in the past but that it is no longer allowed by God in modern times because it would take away freedom of choice in religion, forcing people to believe because of physical proof rather than from a rational consideration examined in freedom.

Being persuaded of the existence of God and the afterlife by physical proof removes from the person the opportunity to raise the perception to spiritual consciousness. What is believed about God in natural-material consciousness wavers and eventually transforms into its opposite. Hence it is that God protects people by making it impossible to have physical proof of Divine and dualist existence. Instead, regeneration and consequent elevation to spiritual consciousness is the only method God makes available for finding proof of Divine existence and dualist eternity. This method insures that the individual not only sees God but loves God. This seeing and loving remains eternal and opens up the life of heaven.

Direct communication or awareness between earthlings and spirits falls into this category. If this conscious experiencing were allowed by God it would provide material proof of dualism and the afterlife. Furthermore, the unequal mental powers of spirits and earthlings would render such communication dangerous to people. The sharing of consciousness directly between people still on earth and those who already departed would remove the freedom of choice and moral responsibility of one's actions here. God who supervises every detail of a human being's life does not permit this since without freedom of choice in moral responsibility the individual cannot be regenerated for a heavenly eternity.

Jung raises the issue of how knowledge is available to human beings, while still on earth and afterwards. He apparently did not work out in his mind how knowledge can be acquired in the afterlife. It is curious that he did not figure out that people as spirits in the afterlife have their own world to get to know and discover, a world that is far more complex than the physical world of nature that they witnessed on earth. The spiritual world is the collective unconscious now made conscious, and Jung knew that this psychic world is without space or other limitation. He apparently did not realize that new knowledge acquisition for spirits is even more essential than natural knowledge acquisition is to people still on earth.

> If there were to be a conscious existence after death, it would, so it seems to me, have to continue on the level of consciousness attained by humanity, which in any age has an upper though variable limit. There are many human beings who throughout their lives and at the moment of death lag behind their

own potentialities and even more important behind the knowledge which has been brought to consciousness by other human beings during their own lifetimes. Hence their demand to attain in death that share of awareness which they failed to win in life. (Jung, *Memories, Dreams, Reflections,* p. 371)

It might be useful to insert here a passage from Swedenborg in which he reports how certain people he met in the afterlife asked him about "*news from earth*":

I was once carried up in my spirit to the heaven of angels, and to one community there. Then some of their wise men came to me asking, 'What is the news from earth?' I told them that the news is that the Lord has revealed secrets far exceeding in excellence any so far revealed since the church began.

'What are these?' they asked. I said that they are:

(1) In every detail the Word contains a spiritual sense corresponding to the natural sense, and by means of that sense the Word forms a link between people in the church and the Lord; it also creates an association with angels, and the holiness of the Word resides in that sense.

(2) The correspondences of which the spiritual sense is composed have been disclosed. 'Did not the inhabitants of the earth,' asked the angels, 'previously know about correspondences?' I told them that they knew nothing at all and these had been lost to sight for thousands of years, in fact, since the time of Job. The people of that and previous ages regarded a knowledge of correspondences as the supreme science, and it was the source of their wisdom, because it was knowledge of spiritual matters to do with heaven and the church. But because the science turned into an idolatrous one, it was by the Lord's Divine providence so wiped out and lost that no one could see any trace of it. Now, however, it has been disclosed by the Lord, so that people belonging to the church may be linked with Him and associated with angels. Both of these take place by means of the Word, every detail of which is a correspondence.

The angels were extremely happy that it has pleased the Lord to reveal this great secret, which has lain so deeply hidden for thousands of years. They said that the reason it was done was in order that the Christian church, which is based upon the Word and is now at its end, should be revived and draw breath from the Lord through heaven. They enquired whether by this science it had been disclosed what was the meaning of baptism and the Holy Supper, which up to now have been the subject of so many speculations. I replied that it had.

(3) I went on to say that at the present time the Lord had made a revelation about people's life after death. 'What about life after death?' said the angels. 'Surely everyone knows that a person lives after death?'

'They do and they do not,' I replied. 'They say that what lives on is not the person, but his soul, and this lives as a spirit. Their notion of a spirit is that it is like the wind or the ether; and they say that the person will only live after Judgment Day. At that time their bodily remains which they left in the world, however eaten away by worms, rats or fish, will be gathered together again and reconstructed to form a body; and this is how people will be brought to life again.'

'What an idea!' said the angels. 'Everyone knows that a person goes on living as a person after death, with the single difference that then he lives as a substantial and not as before as a material person. A substantial person can see another substantial person, just as much as a material person can see another material person. They are unaware of any difference, except that they are in a more perfect state.'

(4) The angels asked, 'What do they know of our world and about heaven and hell?' I replied that they know nothing, but that at the present time the Lord had disclosed what the world is like where the angels and spirits live, and so what heaven and hell are like. It had also been revealed that angels and spirits are linked with human beings, and many other surprising facts. The angels were glad that the Lord had been pleased to disclose such matters, so that mankind should no longer be impelled by ignorance to doubt its own immortality.

(5) I went on to speak of another matter revealed by the Lord at the present time. 'Your world has a different sun from ours. The sun of your world is pure love, the sun of our world is pure fire. Consequently all the radiation from your sun, since it is pure love, has something of life in it; all the radiation from ours, since it is pure fire, has no life in it. This is the origin of the distinction between spiritual and natural, a distinction up to now unknown, which has also been

disclosed. From these facts it has become known what is the source of the light which enlightens the human understanding with wisdom, and what is the source of the heat, which fires the human will with love.

(6) 'In addition it has been disclosed that there are three degrees of life, and that there are consequently three heavens, and a person's mind is divided into those three degrees. A person as a result corresponds to the three heavens.' 'Did they not know this before?' said the angels. I replied that they knew about degrees between greater and less, but nothing about degrees between prior and posterior.

(7) The angel asked whether there had been more revelations than these. I said there had. These were about the Last judgment, and the Lord as being the God of heaven and earth; that God is one both in person and in essence, and in Him is the Divine Trinity, and He is the Lord. Other revelations were about the new church to be established by the Lord and the teaching of that church; about the holiness of the Sacred Scripture; the Book of Revelation too had been revealed; moreover, about the inhabitants of the planets and the other earths elsewhere in the universe. Further many wonders and accounts of experiences had been reported from the spiritual world, by means of which a great deal of wisdom from heaven had been disclosed. (Swedenborg, *True Christian Religion*, 846)

When we depart this life in the physical world we are no longer connected to any source of information regarding events on earth or anywhere in the natural world. Swedenborg reports that everyone goes through a spiritual growth phase after resuscitation whose function is to prepare the person for entry into either a heavenly or hellish psychic society. The person is given experiences of both kind until there is inner realization of one's ultimate character and spiritual destination. When this self-perception is achieved the person knows which way to go next, into a heavenly or hellish community. Whichever choice people make when entering the mental state of heaven or hell, they feel like they've arrived home at last. The other members of that spiritual community appear as friends and family on account of their sharing the same loves and affections that they had on earth.

It is not clear whether Jung picked up these details when reading Swedenborg as a medical student some decades before he wrote about this subject in his later books.

I had another experience of the evolution of the soul after death when about a year after my wife's death I suddenly awoke one night and knew that I had been with her in the south of France, in Provence, and had spent an entire day with her. She was engaged on studies of the Grail there. That seemed significant to me, for she had died before completing her work on this subject. Interpretation on the subjective level that my anima had not yet finished with the work she had to do yielded nothing of interest; I know quite well that I am not yet finished with that. But the thought that my wife was continuing after death to work on her further spiritual development however that may be conceived struck me as meaningful and held a measure of reassurance for me. (Jung, *Memories, Dreams, Reflections*, p. 371)

Swedenborg has the following report to relate about Melanchthon ("one of the leaders of the Protestant Reformation") who was now in the afterlife world. The report shows how Jung's intuition about his wife was actually realistic. Swedenborg's report also shows that when the outer self is different from the inner self, the inner self wins out and determines what choice is made next. It is the inner self that creates one's destiny in eternity.

As for Melanchthon, I have been allowed to learn a number of things about the kind of life he had when he first arrived in the spiritual world and how his circumstances changed later on. I learned this not only from angels but also from some interactions of my own with him. I have spoken with him a number of times, but not as often or as intimately as with Luther. The reason the communication was not as often or as intimate was that he was not in a position to have as much access to me, because in his studies he was fixated on justification by faith alone; he was not focusing on goodwill, and I was surrounded by angelic spirits who were devoted to goodwill, and they blocked his access to me.

I have been told that as soon as he arrived in the spiritual world, there was a house prepared for him that was much like the house where he had lived in the world. In fact, this is done for most newly arrived spirits, with the result that they do not realize they are no longer in the physical world. The time just after they died seems to them in retrospect as if they had merely been asleep.

Everything in his apartment was the same as it had been - the same table, the same writing desk with pigeonholes, the same bookcase. Therefore as soon as he arrived there, he sat down at his table as if he had just woken up from a night's sleep. He continued writing, as he had been, on the subject of justification by faith alone. He wrote on this topic for a number of days without making even the slightest mention of goodwill. The angels noticed this and asked him through messengers why he was not also writing about goodwill.

"Goodwill has nothing to do with the church," he replied. "If it were made out to be some essential attribute of the church, people would take credit for being justified and saved, and this would deprive faith of its spiritual essence."

When the angels who were above his head sensed his answer, and when the angels who were associated with him whenever he left home heard about it, they withdrew from him. (Every new arrival is accompanied by angels to begin with.)

Several weeks after that, the furnishings and supplies in his apartment began to fade away gradually until they disappeared. Eventually, there was nothing left there but a table, some pieces of paper, a pen, and some ink. The walls of his apartment were by then simply plastered with lime, and his floor was made of yellow bricks. He found himself wearing humble clothing. He was very surprised by this, and asked around to find out why this was. He was told that it was because he was removing goodwill from the church when in fact goodwill is the very heart of the church. Every time it came up, however, he strongly disagreed.

He continued to write about faith as the church's only essential ingredient and the only means of being saved, and he kept creating a greater and greater distance between goodwill and the church. Because he did so, he one day suddenly found himself underground in a workhouse where there were others like him. He wanted to leave, but was prevented from doing so. He was informed that this and nothing else was the final outcome for people who threw goodwill and good works out the church door.

Nevertheless, because he had been one of the leaders of the Protestant Reformation, he was released from there by command of the Lord and brought back to his old apartment, where there was nothing but a table, some paper, a pen, and some ink.

Because his ideas were set, he once again filled that paper with the same theological error. Therefore there was no way to prevent him from going down again to his friends in confinement and then coming back up again. When he came back up, he was dressed in hairy animal skins, because faith that lacks goodwill is freezing cold.

He told me firsthand that there was another room off his apartment at the back, where people like him who had likewise banished goodwill were sitting at three tables. A fourth table would sometimes appear there as well, with various kinds of monsters on it, but he and the others were for some reason not frightened away by them. He said he was having conversations with the other people, and every day they were giving him further support for his views.

Quite a while later, fear did take hold of him, and he began writing something about goodwill, but what he would write on a piece of paper one day would no longer be visible the next day. (Actually, this can happen to anyone in that world. What the outer self writes without the compliance of the inner self at the same time; therefore what is written under coercion rather than in freedom spontaneously deletes itself.)

Then the new heaven began to be established by the Lord. In the light from that heaven, Melanchthon began to think that he might actually be in error. He started to feel anxiety about what his final outcome was going to be. He became aware of some deep ideas that had been impressed on him earlier about goodwill. In that state of mind he did some research in the Word. His eyes were opened and he saw that the Word was completely full of loving God and loving our neighbor. He came to see that what the Lord said was true - that all the Law and the Prophets, that is, the Word as a whole, did indeed hinge on these two commandments [Matthew 22:40].

He was then moved to another house much deeper to the south on the western side. He had a conversation with me there, and told me that now his writing about goodwill was not disappearing the way it used to; it would fade somewhat, but it was still legible the following day.

I was surprised by the fact that when he walked, his footsteps made a clanking sound, like someone walking across cobblestones in iron shoes.

To these points I might add that once, when some spirits who had recently arrived from earth came to his apartment to see him and speak with him, he called on one of the magic spirits who had the ability to project images to look like furniture and accessories. That spirit decorated his apartment with apparent wall hangings, carpets with a rose pattern, and a bookcase in the middle of the room. As soon as the visitors left, all that disappeared, though, and the apartment returned to its bare lime-plastered walls and its stark emptiness. But this happened when he was in that first state. (Swedenborg, *True Christian Religion*, n.797)

One can't help wonder whether Jung had read this story and many like it in Swedenborg's Writings, and if not, what his reaction would have been. Would it have made a difference to his spiritual development and the content of his psychology? Jung often wondered publicly about these things. His intuition about the details of the afterlife was extraordinary. In the following passage Jung senses that consciousness raising must occur in "earthly life" and that such as is the person's level of thinking upon death, such will be that person's level of thinking in the afterlife.

> The maximum awareness which has been attained anywhere forms, so it seems to me, the upper limit of knowledge to which the dead can attain. That is probably why earthly life is of such great significance, and why it is that what a human being "brings over" at the time of his death is so important. Only here, in life on earth, where the opposites clash together, can the general level of consciousness be raised. That seems to be man's metaphysical task which he cannot accomplish without "mythologizing." (Jung, *Memories, Dreams, Reflections*, 390)

Jung correctly sees that consciousness can be raised only in the clash of opposites in the mind. Jung does not specify why, but in Swedenborg we read that the operational level of consciousness matches the individual's moral state of mind. Swedenborg connects goodness and mutual love with level of understanding, which rises higher and is more encompassing the greater the perfection of the person's expression and practice of considerateness and love in daily interactions with others.

The anatomy of regeneration requires that it take place prior to death, and it is a process that takes years to progress. Character reversal requires freedom of choice for good or for evil, for love of others as much as self or love of self only. It is necessary that this choice be made in freedom because only in freedom can we choose what we love. In order for character reformation to be permanent we must love the new self and hate the old. Freedom and love must go together.

This freedom to choose is engineered by God by holding the individual's mind in balance between hellish psychic societies and heavenly societies. The balance is the freedom, not the individual. The forces of good and the forces of evil are outside the personality and are not part of the person.

Hence the balance is achieved by external means independent of the individual. In such a state we can choose freely according to our love. By this choice we permanently appropriate the trait to ourselves.

After the dying-resuscitation process the anatomy changes. Now the spiritual body is no longer attached to the physical. It is no longer possible for that spiritual body to be kept in balance such as it was when still attached to the physical body. Now the internal character of the individual surfaces and takes over. There can be no other choice but what that new personality structure will allow. The chief or ruling love arranges all other loves, motives, intentions, and affections into an order below itself and compatible with itself. All else is neutralized and rendered inactive. The new individual is now a caricature of either all good or all bad.

Hence it is that experiencing regeneration is a work that must proceed prior to death. For the selfish person there is no repentance after death, consequently no salvation.

Jung's Near Death Experience

Near Death Experiences or NDEs have been reported by thousands of people. If you search NDEs on the Web you get half a million results. Searching Google Scholar gives you over 10,000 academic research articles and books on NDEs.

A number of NDE reports recently appeared in books and some of them were on the bestseller list. Movies and videos were also made. Millions of people today around the world are familiar with stories or reports of near death experiences. To many people these reports are taken as evidence, even proof, that life after death exists. It is remarkable that the people who have had these experiences acquire an unshakable confidence in the existence of the afterlife and the goodness and love of God.

Thousands of reports of NDE experiences can be found collected on various web sites, e.g.: the *Near Death Experiences Research Foundation* at: http://www.nderf.org/NDERF/NDE_Archives/NDERF_NDEs.htm or the

International Association for Near Death Experiences at:
https://iands.org/about-ndes.html

Here are some examples of what people are chatting about:

> Question: What is our purpose on the other side, do we accomplish anything there? Or do we just simply exist and experience the love and peace. Is there progress in the spirit world?

> Answer: Natalie I never had a NDE, but I have translated so many NDEs and from what I recall, some experiencers told about many other dimensions of existence and of learning. We probably will never get bored. As far as I understand it, this state of being is a state, where what we think about is realizing immediately.

> I came to understand that there are certain things we only can learn when we are here on earth, and one of those things is dealing with time, not getting everything we want immediately. Also learning about what pain and misery is and therefore getting a better understanding of compassion. In a realm where there is no pain and constant happiness this could be somewhat difficult.

> Therefore my understanding is so that we are spirit beings living a short while here on earth and trying to fulfill the goals we set ourselves before we came here.

> +++

> I realize this is an old discussion but it is a concept I've been pondering too.

> As you said, Garry, many NDE experiencers say they are told, "It's not your time." Many NDE experiencers have also said they were asked if they wanted to stay or go back to their bodies/life. Even though a majority chose to stay they are told, "It's not your time" and sent back anyway. What's up with that? Why give them a choice to stay or go back then send them back against their wishes?

> Of course, we'd never hear from those whose choice to stay was granted because they would be dead rather than a NDE experiencer. But why give them a choice at all, why bother with that question in the first place?

And just who is it making these "choices" for us? Some call it "God", others call him/her some supreme being, angels, etc. making these decisions. But how can we die when it's not our time only to be sent back? I mean, what is going on? Did some clerk in the "Time/Not Time" office screw up and zap someone before their time? Are these beings that send people back against their wishes some kind of damage control, PR reps? Can Heaven make mistakes? (I realize I am using earth-bound, human terms to ask questions but there is a point if you read between the lines.)

Again, I am not expecting answers from anyone just seeking further discussion and ideas - bouncing thoughts off each other. I am working on getting a better, more accurate picture of what people are experiencing when they go to this realm/dimension/whatever and working on a way to recognize how NDE's are filtered back and forth between here and there through cultural, spiritual, psychophysiological models, i.e. perceptions.

+++

About the scientific aspect and proof of nde's. I personally have no interest in proof. Proof is not needed for me. I experienced it. There were no questions unanswered. There was absolutely no confusion about anything.

I think it would be wasteful use of ones time to bother looking for concrete evidence. I believe everything does happen as it should, and when and how it should. This is something I understood while 'gone' and I have returned with an inherent trust and knowing of the reality of the these things.

I know scientists have a need to prove things. But, when we get 'there', all is clearly understood...the mystery is solved, so I see no need for proving anything. To me, searching for such proof would take away from time to do important things, like caring for and loving one another.

From: *NDE Research Foundation Forum* at:
http://nderf.me/topic670.html

In his autobiography dictated just before his death in 1961 Jung gives us a report of his near death experience that occurred to him in 1944.

At the beginning of 1944 I broke my foot, and this misadventure was followed by a heart attack. In a state of unconsciousness I experienced deliriums and visions which must have begun when I hung on the edge of death and was being given oxygen and camphor injections. The images were so tremendous that I myself concluded that I was close to death. My nurse afterward told me, "It was as if you were surrounded by a bright glow" That was a phenomenon she had sometimes observed in the dying, she added. I had reached the outermost limit, and do not know whether I was in a dream or an ecstasy. At any rate, extremely strange things began to happen to me.

It seemed to me that I was high up in space. Far below I saw the globe of the earth, bathed in a gloriously blue light. I saw the deep blue sea and the continents. Far below my feet lay Ceylon, and in the distance ahead of me the subcontinent of India. My field of vision did not include the whole earth, but its global shape was plainly distinguishable and its outlines shone with a silvery gleam through that wonderful blue light. In many places the globe seemed colored, or spotted dark green like oxydized silver.

Far away to the left lay a broad expanse the reddish-yellow desert of Arabia; it was as though the silver of the earth had there assumed a reddish-gold hue. Then came the Red Sea, and far, far back as if in the upper left of a map I could just make out a bit of the Mediterranean. My gaze was directed chiefly toward that. Everything else appeared indistinct. I could also see the snow-covered Himalayas, but in that direction it was foggy or cloudy. I did not look to the right at all. I knew that I was on the point of departing from the earth. Later I discovered how high in space one would have to be to have so extensive a view approximately a thousand miles! The sight of the earth from this height was the most glorious thing I had ever seen.

After contemplating it for a while, I turned around. I had been standing with my back to the Indian Ocean, as it were, and my face to the north. Then it seemed to me that I made a turn to the south. Something new entered my field of vision. A short distance away I saw in space a tremendous dark block of stone, like a meteorite. It was about the size of my house, or even bigger. It was floating in space, and I myself was floating in space.

I had seen similar stones on the coast of the Gulf of Bengal. They were blocks of tawny granite, and some of them had been hollowed out into temples. My stone was one such gigantic dark block. An entrance led into a small antechamber. To the right of the entrance, a black Hindu sat silently in lotus posture upon a stone bench. He wore a white gown, and I knew that he expected me. Two steps led up to this antechamber, and inside, on the left, was the gate to the temple. Innumerable tiny niches, each with a saucer-like concavity filled with coconut oil and small burning wicks, surrounded the door with a wreath of bright flames. I had once actually seen this when I visited the Temple of the Holy Tooth at Kandy in Ceylon; the gate had been framed by several rows of burning oil lamps of this sort.

As I approached the steps leading up to the entrance into the rock, a strange thing happened: I had the feeling that everything was being sloughed away; everything I aimed at or wished for or thought, the whole phantasmagoria of earthly existence, fell away or was stripped from me an extremely painful process. Nevertheless something remained; it was as if I now carried along with me everything I had ever experienced or done, everything that had happened around me. I might also say: it was with me, and I was it. I consisted of all that, so to speak. I consisted of my own history, and I felt with great certainty: this is what I am. "I am this bundle of what has been, and what has been accomplished."

This experience gave me a feeling of extreme poverty, but at the same time of great fullness. There was no longer anything I wanted or desired. I existed in an objective form; I was what I had been and lived. At first the sense of annihilation predominated, of having been stripped or pillaged; but suddenly that became of no consequence. Everything seemed to be past; what remained was a fait accompli, without any reference back to what had been. There was no longer any regret that something had dropped away or been taken away. On the contrary: I had everything that I was, and that was everything. Something else engaged my attention: as I approached the temple I had the certainty that I was about to enter an illuminated room and would meet there all those people to whom I belong in reality.

There I would at last understand this too was a certainty what historical nexus I or my life fitted into. I would know what had been before me, why I had come into being, and where my life was flowing. My life as I lived it had often seemed to me like a story that has no beginning and no end. I had the feeling that I was a historical fragment, an excerpt for which the preceding and succeeding text was missing. My life seemed to have been snipped out of a long chain of events, and many questions had remained unanswered. Why had it taken this course? Why had I brought these particular assumptions with me? What had I made of them? What will follow? I felt sure that I would receive an answer to all these questions as soon as I entered the rock temple. There I would learn why everything had been thus and not otherwise. There I would meet the people who knew the answer to my question about what had been before and what would come after.

While I was thinking over these matters, something happened that caught my attention. From below, from the direction of Europe, an image floated up. It was my doctor, Dr. H. or, rather, his likeness framed by a golden chain or a golden laurel wreath. I knew at once: "Aha, this is my doctor, of course, the one who has been treating me. But now he is coming in his primal form, as a basileus of Kos In life he was an avatar of this basileus, the temporal embodiment of the primal form, which has existed from the beginning. Now he is appearing in that primal form".

Presumably I too was in my primal form, though this was something I did not observe but simply took for granted. As he stood before me, a mute exchange of thought took place between us. Dr. H. had been delegated by the earth to deliver a message to me, to tell me that there was a protest against my going away, I had no right to leave the earth and must return. The moment I heard that, the vision ceased.

I was profoundly disappointed, for now it all seemed to have been for nothing. The painful process of defoliation had been in vain, and I was not to be allowed to enter the temple, to join the people in whose company I belonged. In reality, a good three weeks were still to pass before I could truly make up my mind to live again. I could not eat because all food repelled me. The view of city and mountains from my sickbed seemed to me like a painted curtain with black holes in it, or a tattered sheet of newspaper full of photographs that meant nothing. Disappointed, I thought, "Now I must return to the 'box system' again." For I seemed to me as if behind the horizon of the cosmos a three-dimensional world had been artificially built up, in which each person sat by himself in a little box.

And now I should have to convince myself all over again that this was important! Life and the whole world struck me as a prison, and it bothered me beyond measure that I should again be finding all that quite in order. I had been so glad to shed it all, and now it had come about that I along with everyone else would again be hung up in a box by a thread. While I floated in space, I had been weightless, and there had been nothing tugging at me.

And now all that was to be a thing of the past!

I felt violent resistance to my doctor because he had brought me back to life. At the same time, I was worried about him. "His life is in danger, for heaven's sake! He has appeared to me in his primal form! When anybody attains this form it means he is going to die, for already he belongs to the 'greater company'!" Suddenly the terrifying thought came to me that Dr. H. would have to die in my stead. I tried my best to talk to him about it, but he did not understand me. Then I became angry with him. "Why does he always pretend he doesn't know he is a basileus of Kos? And that he has already assumed his primal form? He wants to make me believe that he doesn't know!" That irritated me.

My wife reproved me for being so unfriendly to him. She was right; but at the time I was angry with him for stubbornly refusing to speak of all that had passed between us in my vision. "Damn it all, he ought to watch his step. He has no right to be so reckless! I want to tell him to take care of himself." I was firmly convinced that his life was in jeopardy. In actual fact I was his last patient. On April 4, 1944 I still remember the exact date I was allowed to sit up on the edge of my bed for the first time since the beginning of my illness, and on this same day Dr. H. took to his bed and did not leave it again. I heard that he was having intermittent attacks of fever. Soon afterward he died of septicemia. He was a good doctor; there was something of the genius about him. Otherwise he would not have appeared to me as a prince of Kos.

During those weeks I lived in a strange rhythm. By day I was usually depressed. I felt weak and wretched, and scarcely dared to stir. Gloomily, I thought, "Now I must go back to this drab world." Toward evening I would fall asleep, and my sleep would last until about midnight. Then I would come to myself and lie awake for about an hour, but in an utterly transformed state. It was as if I were in an ecstasy. I felt as though I were floating in space, as though I were safe in the womb of the universe in a tremendous void, but filled with the highest possible feeling of happiness. "This is eternal bliss," I thought. "This cannot be described; it is far too wonderful!" Everything around me seemed enchanted.

At this hour of the night the nurse brought me some food she had warmed for only then was I able to take any, and I ate with appetite. For a time it seemed to me that she was an old Jewish woman, much older than she actually was, and that she was preparing ritual kosher dishes for me. When I looked at her, she seemed to have a blue halo around her head. I myself was, so it seemed, in the Pardes Rimmonim, the garden of pomegranates, and the wedding of Tifereth with Malchuth was taking place.

Or else I was Rabbi Simon ben Jochai, whose wedding in the afterlife was being celebrated. It was the mystic marriage as it appears in the Cabbalistic tradition. I cannot tell you how wonderful it was. I could only think continually, "Now this is the garden of pomegranates! Now this is the marriage of Malchuth with Tifereth!" I do not know exactly what part I played in it. At bottom it was I myself: I was the marriage. And my beatitude was that of a blissful wedding.

Gradually the garden of pomegranates faded away and changed. There followed the Marriage of the Lamb, in a Jerusalem festively bedecked. I cannot describe what it was like in detail. These were ineffable states of joy. Angels were present, and light. I myself was the "Marriage of the Lamb."

That, too, vanished, and there came a new image, the last vision. I walked up a wide valley to the end, where a gentle chain of hills began. The valley ended in a classical amphitheater. It was magnificently situated in the green landscape. And there, in this theater, the hierosgamos was being celebrated. Men and women dancers came onstage, and upon a flower-decked couch All-father Zeus and Hera consummated the mystic marriage, as it is described in the Iliad.

All these experiences were glorious. Night after night I floated in a state of purest bliss, "thronged round with images of all creation." Gradually, the motifs mingled and paled. Usually the visions lasted for about an hour; then I would fall asleep again. By the time morning drew near, I would feel: Now gray morning is coming again; now comes the gray world with its boxes! What idiocy, what hideous nonsense! Those inner states were so fantastically beautiful that by comparison this world appeared downright ridiculous. As I approached closer to life again, they grew fainter, and scarcely three weeks after the first vision they ceased altogether.

It is impossible to convey the beauty and intensity of emotion during those visions. They were the most tremendous things I have ever experienced. And what a contrast the day was: I was tormented and on edge; everything irritated me; everything was too material, too crude and clumsy, terribly limited both spatially and spiritually. It was all an imprisonment, for reasons impossible to divine, and yet it had a kind of hypnotic power, a cogency, as if it were reality itself, for all that I had clearly perceived its emptiness. Although my belief in the world returned to me, I have never since entirely freed myself of the impression that this life is a segment of existence which is enacted in a three-dimensional boxlike universe especially set up for it.

There is something else I quite distinctly remember. At the beginning, when I was having the vision of the garden of pomegranates, I asked the nurse to forgive me if she were harmed. There was such sanctity in the room, I said, that it might be harmful to her. Of course she did not understand me. For me the presence of sanctity had a magical atmosphere; I feared it might be unendurable to others. I understood then why one speaks of the odor of sanctity, of the "sweet smell" of the Holy Ghost. This was it. There was a pneuma of inexpressible sanctity in the room, whose manifestation was the mysterium coniunctionis.

I would never have imagined that any such experience was possible. It was not a product of imagination. The visions and experiences were utterly real; there was nothing subjective about them; they all had a quality of absolute objectivity.

We shy away from the word "eternal," but I can describe the experience only as the ecstasy of a non-temporal state in which present, past, and future are one. Everything that happens in time had been brought together into a concrete whole. Nothing was distributed over time, nothing could be measured by temporal concepts.

The experience might best be defined as a state of feeling, but one which cannot be produced by imagination. How can I imagine that I exist simultaneously the day before yesterday, today, and the day after tomorrow? There would be things which would not yet have begun, other things which would be indubitably present, and others again which would already be finished and yet all this would be one. The only thing that feeling could grasp would be a sum, an iridescent whole, containing all at once expectation of a beginning, surprise at what is now happening, and satisfaction or disappointment with the result of what has happened. One is interwoven into an indescribable whole and yet observes it with complete objectivity.

Jung's near death experience in 1944 was one of the first such experiences to be recorded and published. There are many similarities in Jung's description of his experience and those being reported today. A central feature of such experiences is that they are "glorious" and occur in a mental state of "floating in pure bliss". Further, since it is a "near" death experience, not a death experience, there is the injunction that the person must "go back" and this is experienced with great regret, disappointment, and in the case of Jung, depression. Finally, the experience is felt as "objective" and overwhelmingly "real" rather than an imagined fantasy or vision. Here is a summary of Jung's description that highlight these facts:

> Earthly existence, fell away or was stripped from me. There was no longer any regret that something had dropped away or been taken away. I had everything that I was, and that was everything. Disappointed, I thought, "Now I must return to the 'box system' again." For I seemed to me as if behind the horizon of the cosmos a three-dimensional world had been artificially built up, in which each person sat by himself in a little box. Gloomily, I thought, "Now I must go back to this drab world." Or else I was Rabbi Simon ben Jochai, whose wedding in the afterlife was being celebrated. It was the mystic marriage as it appears in the Cabbalistic tradition. I cannot tell you how wonderful it was.

> All these experiences were glorious. Night after night I floated in a state of purest bliss, "thronged round with images of all creation." Gradually, the motifs mingled and paled. It is impossible to convey the beauty and intensity of emotion during those visions. They were the most tremendous things I have ever experienced. I would never have imagined that any such experience was possible. It was not a product of imagination. The visions and experiences were utterly real; there was nothing subjective about them; they all had a quality of absolute objectivity. We shy away from the word "eternal," but I can describe the experience only as the ecstasy of a non-temporal state in which present, past, and future are one.

It is instructive to compare Jung's near death experience with Swedenborg's repeated experience of the dying-resuscitation process that is presented in the preceding section. The following is a summary of Swedenborg's description:

(1) Death occurs when the respiration and heartbeat both stop. The physical body in this world is then separated from the spiritual body in the afterlife,

which is then left to itself.

(2) Resuscitation means the drawing forth of the spirit from the body, and its introduction into the spiritual world.

(3) Swedenborg observed the process of resuscitation with many others, and himself had the actual experience so *"that I might have a complete knowledge of the process"*.

(4) When physical respiration ceases one becomes conscious of the inner respiration of the spiritual body. Thinking and perception continue without interruption.

(5) One becomes conscious of angels at a distance, then close by sitting by the head. Their feelings and thoughts are communicated and experienced. The person undergoing resuscitation is not aware of his or her own emotions or concerns.

(6) For several hours the angels hold the person in the same thoughts as when dying. Afterwards the person is awakened and gradually takes over control, coming into the familiar affections and thoughts that were habitual prior to death.

(7) The eyes then open. The person now conscious with the spiritual body walks away from the resuscitation zone and begins a new continuation in eternal life, meeting others who are already in the afterlife and with whom they have interactions and relationships.

It is clear that the near death experiences (NDEs) of Jung and others are of a different nature than the actual dying process that Swedenborg was allowed to experience several times. With NDEs the person comes back to life on earth. With actual dying the person awakens from the resuscitation process and can no longer come back. NDEs function psychologically to elevate the person's consciousness into a mental state of extreme happiness and absolute confidence. On the other hand the actual dying-resuscitation experience seems to occur without the emotional involvement and psychological elevation. It is clear from the Swedenborg reports that near death experiences are not at all similar to the experience of actually dying,

God, Immortality and Theistic Psychology Series
by Dr. Leon James

Jung and Swedenborg on God and Life After Death (2015) (current book)

Biology of Consciousness and Immortality: Knowledge That Holds the Key to Our Eternal Destiny in the Afterlife (forthcoming)

Discovering the Spiritual Psychology of Jung and Swedenborg (forthcoming)

Theistic Psychology Hidden in the Bible (forthcoming)

Experiencing Regeneration: Equipping Our Personality For Living In The Afterlife (2015)
(Print and Kindle Digital versions at Amazon.com)

The Conjoined Pair: Natural and Spiritual Marriage (2012)
(Print at amazon.com)

The Correspondential Sense of Sacred Scriptures: Proving that there is a Unified Theistic Psychology Hidden within the World's Historical Sacred Writings (2009)
On the web: http://www.theisticpsychology.org/books/ssss.htm

Best Friends in Love and Together Forever: The Natural and Spiritual Dimension of Marriage (2008)
On the web: http://theisticpsychology.org/books/best-friends-in-love.htm

Principles of Theistic Psychology: The Scientific Knowledge of God Extracted from the Correspondential Sense of Sacred Scripture (18

Volumes) (2004-2008)
On the web: http://theisticpsychology.org/books/theistic/index.htm

A Man of the Field: Forming the New Church Mind in Today's World (3
Volumes) (2002-2014)
(Print and Kindle version at amazon.com)

Moses, Paul, and Swedenborg: Three Steps in Rational Spirituality (1999)
On the web: http://theisticpsychology.org/books/rationality/moses.html

Swedenborg Encyclopedia of Theistic Psychology: The Ideas of
Emanuel Swedenborg (1668-1772) Expressed In Modern Scientific
Psychology (1995-2010) (multiple Volumes)
On the web: http://theisticpsychology.org/gloss.html

www.ingramcontent.com/pod-product-compliance
Lightning Source LLC
Chambersburg PA
CBHW062002280526
45787CB00005B/1965